RAHUL DRAVID

A BIOGRAPHY

INDIA
PEPSI

RAHUL DRAVID

A BIOGRAPHY

VEDAM JAISHANKAR

UBSPD
UBS Publishers' Distributors Pvt. Ltd.
New Delhi • Bangalore • Kolkata • Chennai
Patna • Bhopal • Ernakulam • Mumbai

UBS Publishers' Distributors Pvt. Ltd.
5 Ansari Road, **New Delhi-110 002**
Phones: 011-23273601-04, 23266646
Fax: 23276593, 23274261
E-mail: ubspd@ubspd.com

10 First Main Road, Gandhi Nagar, **Bangalore-560 009**
Phones: 080-2253903, 2263901, 2263902 • Fax: 2263904
E-mail: ubspdbng@eth.net

8/1-B, Chowringhee Lane, **Kolkata-700 016**
Phones: 033-22521821, 22522910, 22529473 • Fax: 22523027
E-mail: ubspdcal@cal.vsnl.net.in

60, Nelson Manickam, Aminjikarai, **Chennai-600 029**
Phones: 044-23746222, 23746351-2 • Fax: 23746287
E-mail: ubspd@che.ubspd.com

5 A, Rajendra Nagar, **Patna-800 016**
Phones: 0612-2672856, 2673973, 2686170 • Fax: 2686169
E-mail: ubspdpat1@sancharnet.in

143 M P Nagar, Zone I, **Bhopal-462 011**
Phones: 0755-5203183, 5203193, 2555228 • Fax: 2555285
E-mail: ubspdbhp@sancharnet.in

No. 40/7940, Convent Road, **Ernakulam-682 035**
Phones: 0484-2353901, 2363905 • Fax: 2365511
E-mail: ubspdchn@eth.net

2nd floor Apeejay Chambers,
5 Wallace Street, Fort, **Mumbai-400 001**
Phones: 56376922, 56376923 • Fax: 56376921
E-mail: ubspdmum@mum.ubspd.com

Visit us at www.ubspd.com & www.gobookshopping.com

First Published 2004

Cover & Book Design: Dushyant Parasher

Cover photo: Pradeep Mandhani

Processed and Printed by
Nutech Photolithographers, Delhi

To my mother, who continues to be shocked that any sensible person would want to be a journalist, and my dear wife, Devika

Foreword

It has always surprised me that in a cricket-mad country like ours, where cricketers are such public heroes, there are few good biographies of the players. On the surface of it, there is very little that is not known about the players, so intense is the media attention on them. But few writers have joined the dots to present a whole human being. The good writers on the game in the country (with some exceptions) have preferred the columns of the newspapers to air their views. Increasingly, the space being made available to them has been getting smaller; hence much of significance is being missed out. This biography is important for two reasons. For its subject matter, Rahul Dravid, who is a most articulate and intelligent player, and for its biographer, Vedam Jaishankar, a cricket writer who has known his subject from a very young age.

I have known both since their school days, and I take pride in the fact that each has reached the highest level in his chosen field. Rahul has always been an extremely focused lad, level-headed, and with a finely developed sense of man management. None of us who knew him in the early days is surprised at his steady climb to the top rung of the ladder. He is a good student of the game; but that is not all. He also shows a willingness to learn at all times. This is what sets him apart from his contemporaries. He is the ideal icon for youngsters, especially since he takes time off when he is in Bangalore to speak to them at various levels.

Rahul is an old-fashioned cricketer—God Bless him for that—which means that he plays the game in the spirit in which it ought to be played, and sees himself as an ambassador of his country wherever he plays. A quarter of a century ago, in my playing days, these virtues were taken for granted, and elders drilled it into our heads that cricket was more than a game. Rahul didn't need anything to be drilled into him. He is a natural, both as a player and, in a larger sense, as a representative of a great game. I doubt if any writer knows Rahul as well as Jaishankar does. Like Rahul, he too is a rarity in his field—a balanced writer who is a good student of the game. It has helped that Jaishankar has played cricket himself. Subject and writer are well matched, and that alone makes what you are about to read special.

Brijesh Patel*

---

*Brijesh Patel played 21 Tests for India and scored a century against the West Indies in West Indies. He is a shrewd thinker of the game. Till recently he was the chairman of the National Selection Committee. He is the Secretary of the Karnataka State Cricket Association, a member of the Board of Control for Cricket in India and the Director of the National Cricket Academy.

Preface

The first time I saw Rahul Sharad Dravid was in the late 1980s. At that time I was a journalist with *The Indian Express* in Bangalore. Rahul, along with a couple of his school teammates, had come to the office with scores of his inter-school match and wanted them published. He was nervous, but spoke very well even then.

Those days, we in *The Indian Express* took great pride in our local cricket reporting. We would go from ground to ground and watch school cricket, junior age-group cricket, senior division league matches or any match where a youngster of any potential played. Of course, playing the game helped keep in close touch with local cricket circles and we instantly heard of any promising cricketer coming through the pipeline.

Thus, when I heard of this stylish youngster of impeccable technique and soon met him at my office, we, at *The Indian Express*, marked him out as one of the promising players and watched out for him in the junior games. Of course, we had drawn a list of a dozen young players to follow and some of them, Sujith Somasundar, Fazal Khaleel, J Arunkumar, Yere Goud, Valmik Buch, went on to play first-class cricket. Rahul, with more talent, ambition, drive and discipline than all of them, went much further.

Rahul looked 'every inch a cricketer' even at that young age. He always wore spotless white clothes to nets and matches, and this straightaway made him stand out from the rest.

Born 11 January, 1973 in Indore, Rahul's rapid development as a cricketer came in his late teens. I remember staying back in Goa after a one-day international match between India and Sri Lanka just to watch some of the cream of Karnataka youngsters, including Rahul, play in a Ghulam Ahmed Trophy under-19 game. Most of them—Rahul, Sujith,

Fazal—had a successful outing with the bat. But when it came to bowling, they found that the Goans were not too keen on throwing away their wickets. The Karnataka Manager, AV Venkatnarayan, former Ranji Trophy player, was very tense and fretting and fuming as the Goans defended stoutly. Suddenly Sujith, the Karnataka skipper, threw the ball to Rahul who bowled steadily to pick up three quick wickets. Karnataka, thus, forced Goa to follow on.

Although I had followed Rahul's initial career pretty closely, I was surprised when he was asked to bowl. In fact, it was the first time I had seen him do it. When I mentioned this to Venkatnarayan, he remarked: "That boy can do anything if he makes up his mind. He can bat, bowl, keep wickets and he is also very intelligent. I only hope he does not grow up getting confused with all these things he is doing."

* * *

Tales of Rahul's bowling ability flowed from former St Anthony's Boys School students. One recalled how Rahul while in class three led St Anthony's against their old boys. The old boys were all drawn from the fifth standard of St Joseph's Boys School and led by Sandeep Somesh who later went on to become an Olympian and played hockey for India. Rahul, besides scoring a few runs, captured eight Josephite wickets. He also broke one stump while bowling. To this day that souvenir is treasured by St Anthony's Boys School.

More recently, Rahul was the chief guest at a 5-a-side hockey tournament. Sandeep Somesh recalled how Rahul used to play excellent hockey and was alongside him in the forward line of the St Joseph's Boys High School team (St Anthony's students moved to St Joseph's after third standard). "I am lucky he took up cricket. Otherwise I would never have played hockey for India," said Somesh while welcoming Rahul to the function. Rahul, never short for words, in his reply said: "What most of you don't know is that Sandeep used to play cricket for the school team. Luckily he gave up cricket and concentrated on hockey. Otherwise I would not have made the Indian team!"

Rahul's sense of humour surfaces every now and then. While working on this biography I told him once that I found it eerie that all the people I spoke to had only good things to say about him. "What is this magic charm you've worked on everybody," I asked him. Pat came his reply: "Come on Vedam. If you speak only to my friends what else do you expect? You must get hold of some of my enemies. They'll give you more ammunition than you can handle!"

***

Cricketers by and large are a selfish lot. They are self-centred and grab whatever they can for themselves. Of course, when they are in the limelight and do well everybody wants a glimpse of them. The hangers-on bask in the reflected glory. But once their playing days are over, these same hangers-on come out with horrific stories about the cricketers.

But Rahul is one of the few cricketers on whom the muck will not stick. In many ways he is a very rare type of cricketer. Rahul has tremendous regard and time for his employers in Chennai, India Cements. They employed him when he was a teenager and had just broken into first-class cricket. Former India Cricketer VB Chandrasekhar was instrumental in identifying him as a potential player for India Cements. Subsequently, Rahul received tremendous support and encouragement from the Managing Director, Srinivasan. Kasi Vishwanath, another employee of the company, and Dr Natarajan were others who helped him.

When his father Sharad Dravid had a heart operation in Chennai, it was India Cements that rolled out all the support from choosing the hospital and doctor to getting cricketers, umpires and students from Guru Nanak College to donate blood. Rahul, who is the manager (marketing) of the company, never forgot this help. To this day if he is around he makes it a point to turn out for them in league matches. Even if he has just returned from a tough international tour Rahul still ensures that he plays for them. There were times when he would board the overnight train to Chennai, play the match and return to Bangalore. Rahul holds that when he was a nobody they helped him. It was his turn therefore to repay all the help they had rendered. In fact, Rahul has extended this logic even to some of his sponsors who backed him when he was just a first-class player. This is so unlike many others who would not even remember people who had helped them the previous day.

***

Much after Rahul broke into the Ranji Trophy team he played in a Board-recognised private tournament run in the summer by the Brijesh Patel Cricket Academy at the ASC grounds. The numerous players of the camp were asked to report one morning and there was a big melee. The players were all asked to fall in a line till they were sorted into different camp teams. Then the cricket consultant, former Test cricketer GR Vishwanath, walked down the line. Suddenly, on seeing Rahul also in the line he was shocked. "You don't need to fall in line. You relax here," he said and pointed to a bench under a tree. Vishy turned round and said to me: "See how humble he is. Any other Ranji Trophy player would have made sure everybody around was aware of his presence and would have put on airs. I really like the way Rahul does not get worked up about non-issues and stays focused on the job. He has the mind of a winner."

***

Indeed, right through when I worked on this book, I was again and again drawn to Rahul's tough mental make-up. Everybody spoke of his dedication, focus, commitment and sincerity. Rahul's logic was that there are things within his control, like his game, and he could work on it. But then there were also things that fell outside his control, like for instance, the weather. He would not break his head over trying to sort it. He thus had a very clear concept of what he would do and what he could not. His devotion to *yoga* and breathing techniques was in pursuit of his excellence in cricket. Anything that interfered with that pursuit he shunned. This included partying or hitting town on the night before a match.

For me the writing of this biography of Rahul has been an eye-opener. I thought I knew him from the time he was a kid. But as I got deeper into the subject I found that there are many more dimensions to the man. I think his potential is truly fascinating and I eagerly look forward to the day when he would push it to its furthest extent.

Acknowledgements

When UBSPD asked me to write the biography of Rahul Dravid, I jumped at the proposal. I thought it would be a breeze. After all, his principal at school and college and some of his teachers had taught me ten years earlier, I reasoned. His coach Keki Tarapore had also coached me. I had followed his career from the time he was a mere teenager. But when the actual interviewing, meeting, checking on records, archives and, of course, writing came about, I learnt to appreciate how difficult it would have been without a whole lot of support and help.

Rahul, as usual, was outstanding. I would call him up when he was in Scotland, meet him when he was in Bangalore and make phone calls when he was playing elsewhere. His parents, Sharad and Pushpa, too made my task all the easier.

Another great support was KR Gururaja Rao. He was the first from India to be made member of the Association of Cricket Statisticians and Historians in England. He has been providing cricket statistics for All India Radio and Doordarshan since 1979. Gururaja Rao provided all the statistics for this book. He churned out pages after pages of statistics about Rahul Dravid in a jiffy. It turned out that he was one of the first of his tribe to make use of the computer to store and generate statistics.

Brijesh Patel who wrote the Foreword for this book is another dear friend. I have picked his cricket brains from the time I was in school and playing for his club Swastic Union. He continues to be a great help and source of inspiration.

Suresh Menon, fellow journalist and another dear friend, has been an inspiration and support in more ways than even he would know.

Father Dennis Coelho, Father Walter Anrade and Father Eugene Lobo—my former principals and teachers—are still out there and were ever willing to guide and help.

My wife Devika helped me in my own trip of self-discovery. It was satisfying and quite a revelation to know that I was capable of 12 and 14-hour days. Devika put up with my idiosyncrasies during the period. I must acknowledge my young son Arjun's contribution. He answered all the phone calls and also put up with all my books and study material spilling over to his desk.

I must also acknowledge the excellent work of my publishers—UBSPD. But for their constant pushing me for chapters, statistics and the like I doubt whether I could have finished this book in such a short time. Then there is my former colleague and long-distance friend Gulu Ezeikel. But for his prodding and pushing I would not have got down to writing this book.

Finally, my thanks are due to the cricketers, journalists, administrators and teachers who spared time and related all those lovely Rahul Dravid anecdotes.

Contents

Chapter 1

Oh, What a Match!

There is no venue in world cricket more stirring and, at times, daunting than Eden Gardens, Kolkata. The 120,000 spectators that throng the stadium for any major event are passionate, vocal and often explosive. They can lift the morale of a player or team, but at their worst they can also be bizarre and repugnant.

Cricketing greats like Sunil Gavaskar have at times got the worst from the crowd. At one stage, after he was spat at, had rubbish thrown at him and been booed, he swore never to play at the Eden Gardens again. The crowd's wrath also forced the 1996 World Cup semi-final between India and Sri Lanka to be abandoned after the Indian team belied their expectations by playing miserably. In 1999 they again turned violent in the Test against Pakistan. So much so the stadium had to be cleared and the final day's play completed in front of empty stands.

Into this cauldron whose spectators have much in common with the bloodthirsty crowds that thronged the gladiatorial arena of Rome in a bygone era, Australia engaged India in a Test that they thought would underline their superiority as world champions.

The Australians had won a record-breaking 16 Tests in a trot. They had won cricket series everywhere before embarking on a tour to India which Skipper Steve Waugh described as 'the final frontier' for his side. He had thereby hung a label on the Indian team who now had the additional pressure of having to live up to it. The Aussies had already won the first Test of that 2000-2001 series in Mumbai by 10 wickets. They looked supremely confident while India, after series loses to Australia in Australia and to South Africa in India, had only wins against lowly Bangladesh and a home win against Zimbabwe to show.

The Australians, batting first, ran up an impressive total of 445. Skipper Waugh (110) held the lower order batsmen together after Mathew Hayden (97) had done his bit at the top. The talking point of the innings, though, was a hat-trick by Harbhajan Singh. The off-spinner got rid of Ricky Ponting, Adam Gilchrist and Shane Warne with three deliveries of his 16th over to become the first Indian to register a hat-trick in Test cricket.

The Indian reply to Australia's 445 was anything but inspiring. Sadagopan Ramesh (0), Shiv Sundar Das (20) and batting maestro Sachin Tendulkar (10) left early. Rahul Dravid, batting at his customary number three position battled hard for close to two hours before he was deceived and bowled by leg spinner Shane Warne. Skipper Saurav Ganguly was dismissed for 23 and by close of play on the second day, India, at 128 for eight, were in doldrums. The Hyderabadi duo of VVS Laxman (26) and Venkatpathy Raju (3) held fort at close.

Early on the third day, Raju departed before Laxman found an ally in Venkatesh Prasad (7 n.o.). Laxman attacked the bowling in fluent style and made 59 before succumbing to a poor decision by Umpire Peter Willey. India, all out for 171, were asked to follow on. Laxman had batted beautifully in the morning. He had stroked the ball well and was timing it marvelously before being given out, caught off the forearm.

India, following on, batted in aggressive fashion in the second innings as Ramesh played some fine strokes to rattle 30 off 33 balls. But after lunch it was a disaster again for the home side. Ramesh edged Warne to slip. Instead of Rahul, who usually batted at number three, Skipper Saurav sent in Laxman who had already had a good look at the bowling that morning. Saurav also wanted an in-form batsman to keep up the momentum. He was not disappointed. Laxman, playing perhaps the finest innings of his career, timed his strokes handsomely. At the best of times Laxman has been a great timer of the ball and this was the best of times as far as he was concerned.

Unfortunately, though, India lost SS Das (39) when he stepped on his wicket and Sachin (10) when he snicked a delivery to the wicketkeeper. The fall of these wickets drove a whole lot of disgusted Indian fans to get out of the stadium at tea. Who could blame them?

India, trailing by 274 runs and following on, were reduced to 115 for three. And those three batsmen dismissed included Sachin Tendulkar, the destroyer of the Australians on their previous tour to India.

Laxman and Saurav (48) batted fluently to add 117 runs for the fourth wicket before the skipper succumbed. At 232 for four India were stuck on disaster street. This brought in Rahul.

Rahul had had a poor tour of Australia the previous winter, aggregating just 93 runs in three Tests. He had done marginally better in the home series against South Africa. The season had been a poor one for him. But the next season, in the matches preceding the Australian series, he had struck form once again. He had scores of 200 not out (his first double hundred in Tests) and 70 not out in the Delhi Test against Zimbabwe, 162 against them in the next Test in Nagpur and was therefore in good nick.

However, there were elements in the media whose biased pen wrote nasty things about him. There was also a television commentator who probably believed that Rahul edged him out of the Indian team and hence struggled to say anything good about him. Under these circumstances, the two huge scores he had just made in the two Tests before the home series against Australia were either ignored or forgotten. The whole scenario was being built up into a VVS Laxman vs Rahul Dravid battle for the number three slot and a place in the playing eleven.

But Rahul had survived conniving people earlier. Under siege now from a section of the print media and from some of those chatterers on television, he was walking out to do battle, not just for Indian pride, but also his berth in the Indian team. He applauded as Laxman got to the magical three-figure mark and then hung on till the end of the third day. Laxman, at close, was batting on 109 and Rahul was on seven. The spectators at the mammoth Eden Gardens had dwindled to less than 50,000 towards the draw of stumps.

Resuming the innings on the fourth day at 254 for four, Laxman and Rahul had to first weather the second new ball on a pitch livened by early morning dew. The Aussie pacemen, Glen McGrath, Jason Gillespe and Michael Kasprowicz, were hurling everything they had at the batsmen in the hope of finishing off the Test as quickly as possible. But in front of less than 50,000 spectators Rahul showed how dogged and determined he could be. With Laxman exhibiting his silken touch every now and then the Indian duo first passed the 274-mark, ensuring that the Aussies would have to bat again. They then concentrated on seeing the new ball off.

"Batting with Laxman was easy. We have played so much of cricket together, right from the under-19 level that we know each others' game and thinking pretty well. We just decided to go along and not do anything stupid. We'd take it one over at a time and make them earn our wicket, we decided," recalled Rahul.

The duo saw off the second new ball, the follow-on target, the first hour of play and went into lunch at 376 for four. Laxman had added 62 runs to his overnight 109 and Rahul 43 to his score of seven. The morning session had yielded 122 runs, largely owing to the open spaces left in the outfield by the Australians' attacking field positions. Laxman and Rahul were also timing their strokes well. India were now 102 runs to the good and the crowds were trickling in again.

By tea nobody was in doubt that they were witnessing history being made. The Indians had still not lost a wicket as Laxman and Rahul played sensational cricket. The former had reached his double hundred and was on the threshold of passing Sunil Gavakar's 236—the highest by an Indian in Tests. Rahul reached his century, a stupendous one by any yardstick, and then in a rare show of emotion, stripped off his helmet and aggressively waved the bat at the commentator's box. He was not only acknowledging the cheers of the Eden Gardens crowd but also emphasising to those in the media box who had said and written nonsense about him that he was very much around and batting like a champion.

At close on the fourth day, the Aussies were a troubled lot. They were the only team in the history of the game to enforce the follow-on and twice lose Tests. It now seemed like this world champion side was hurtling towards their country's third such defeat. Laxman and Rahul had added 335 runs in a whole day's play without being separated. Laxman was unbeaten on 275 and Rahul on 155. The famed Aussie attack of McGrath, Gillespe, Kasprowicz and Warne had not bagged a single wicket in a whole day's play. The pitch was showing increasing signs of cracking up, yet Warne was driven and cut at will by Laxman and Rahul.

On the last morning a capacity crowd turned up at the Eden Gardens. They knew they would witness history being made on the day. Nobody had any doubts that this was the day the wheels would come off the Aussies' superb record of 16 straight Test wins. Laxman and Rahul added 376 runs for the fifth wicket before Laxman departed in search of quick runs. Rahul made an excellent, combative 180 before being run out. India declared at 657 for seven, leaving the Aussies to make 384 off 75 overs.

They did not have a ghost of a chance on a deteriorating pitch. The top three batsmen in the batting order, Mathew Hayden, Michael Slater and Justin Langer, made a few runs to keep the side in with a chance to draw the Test. But after tea the off spin of Harbhajan and the leg spin of Sachin Tendulkar proved too much and Australia lost by a whopping margin of 171 runs.

Laxman (59 and 282 runs) and Harbhajan (7 and 6 wickets) covered themselves with glory for that stupendous Test victory. India continued to be the 'Final Frontier' for Steve Waugh's Australians. But more than all these, the man who epitomised the spirit of the Indian team on that distant day was the very person the world called 'The Wall'. Rahul Dravid showed yet again that in crunch situations he had no peers in this Indian team. He was the one who would put up his hand and be counted, again and again.

Chapter 2

The Journey of the Dravids

The journey of the Dravids began a long time ago. Vishwanath Haridas Dravid, paternal grandfather of Rahul Dravid, was a professor of Sanskrit (widely accepted as the mother of all Indian languages) at Victoria College, Gwalior. Vishwanath Haridas' grandfather, a Tamilian Iyer (Hindu Brahmin) from a village near Tanjavur—a district of Tamil Nadu state famous for its temples and often referred to as the rice granary of South India—migrated to Gwalior to take up employment as a Brahmin high priest under the Peshwas and Marathas, the rulers of erstwhile Madhya Bharat.

Those days, quite a few South Indian priests migrated to the North to serve under the various kings and rulers of the many princely states that dotted North India. Vishwanath Haridas' grandfather was one such priest.

The movement from Tanjavur in South India to Gwalior in North India called for quite a few adjustments on the part of the Iyer priest. One of these was to sport a new name. For, in North India, the order of the day was to be referred by a surname. In the South, rather than a surname the use of initials against the name was common practice.

Usually, a person adopted his village's name as his surname. This helped indicate his place of origin to all those who came in contact with him.

Unfortunately, not too many in the North were aware of the lifestyle in South India. And even fewer had heard of tiny Tanjavur which was buried way down in the South. Thus when it came for the Peshwas' priest from near Tanjavur to take a surname, the Gwalior residents simply referred to him as Dravidian—the theory being that those South of the Vindhyas mountain range were Dravidians, supposedly the original inhabitants of India, and those in the North were of Aryan stock.

Without getting into the merits or demerits of this theory, the orthodox Iyer Brahmin priest from Tanjavur, the very antithesis of the Dravidian movement which was to sweep Tamil Nadu in subsequent years, was ironically given the surname Dravid (short for Dravidian).

Subsequently, his grandson Vishwanath Haridas Dravid who rose to become the professor of Sanskrit, fathered eleven children—seven sons and four daughters. Sharad Dravid, father of Rahul Dravid, was Vishwanath Haridas' fifth son. Sharad grew up and had his schooling in Indore.

"Everybody spoke Marathi in Gwalior and Indore those days," said Sharad Dravid of his early years. "My parents spoke Tamil, as did my elder brothers. But the younger elements in my family were slowly drifting away from our roots and increasingly assimilating with Marathis and their culture.

"Two of my sisters-in-law are Tamilians but the rest of us were increasingly imbibing everything Maharashtrian. The others in my family, including me, married Maharashtrians. Of course, I still have close relatives who sport Iyer as surname and are now settled in Benares and Jaipur.

"So dominant was Tamilian influence even up to my generation that the *mangalsutra* (bridal necklace equivalent of wedding ring in Western culture) my mother presented my wife is of Tamilian style. Despite the predominance of Tamilian upbringing at home, our awareness level of other South Indian languages like Malayalam, Kannada and Telugu in those days was very negligible. It was only after Indian states were reorganised on the basis of language in 1956 that we become aware of a whole lot of languages of the South," said Sharad Dravid.

His wife, Pushpa Dravid, mother of Rahul and Vijay, belonged to an orthodox Marathi family. She grew up with her three brothers. Her father, a doctor, was psychiatrist in the Gwalior Mental Hospital.

It was, perhaps, from her that Rahul inherited the gift of rigidly compartmentalising his various activities as we shall see later. For Pushpa, revealing tremendous ambition, purpose and self-confidence, took up studying two courses simultaneously at college. Early morning she attended an arts college which was affiliated to the JJ School of

Arts, Bombay. During regular hours she went to the Kamala Raja College. Again in the evening she returned to the arts college. Subsequently, her outstanding time management and determination were to pay off as she walked away with a double postgraduation. Considering that this was during an era when women were seldom allowed the freedom to pursue even a single graduation degree, Pushpa's achievement was nothing short of remarkable.

During this period, Sharad did his BSc in agriculture from the College of Agriculture in Gwalior. Four of his brothers did a stint in the army through the Short Services Commission. This was during the Second World War when there was a pressing need for personnel in the Indian army.

Sharad's elder brother Col KV Dravid was probably the inspiration for the rest of the brothers to take to cricket. He played for Holkar, and later for Services. Col KV Dravid, who was a left-arm spinner, had the distinction of playing with and against such stalwarts as the legendary Col CK Nayudu, his brother CS Nayudu, Mustaq Ali and CT Sarwate.

"My brother was a very good player. Though all of us took to the game, he was the one who went on to play big cricket," recalled Sharad Dravid.

Runs in the Family

Long before Rahul set the national stage alight with his runs, his father Sharad was making an impression with the bat in Indore, Gwalior and Agra.

Turning out for his college team in Gwalior against Holkar College, Indore, he played against Raj Singh Dungarpur, Hanumath Singh, his brother Suryaveer Singh and others. Of course, later they played together, first for Agra University and later for Vikram University.

"My cousin Chandu Dravid, who was in the army, was a very close friend of Raj Singh. They played a lot together at Indore. He passed away sometime back. But even now, whenever I meet Raj Singh he enquires about Chandu's family. Raj Singh and I ran into each other only during the inter-college matches as I studied in Gwalior and he in Indore. But later we represented the same university," said Sharad who used to bat in the top order and often opened the batting.

Those were the days when playing technically correct cricket was more important than throwing the bat around and edging and lofting a few boundaries. Sharad, an open admirer of Vijay Hazare's classical style of batting, modelled himself after his hero.

"I would only play the ball along the ground. I would never loft the ball. In any case those days people believed only lousy batsmen lofted the ball. I scored a couple of centuries for the university, but I seldom played the ball in the air. The fielding and catching in the old days were never as good as they are these days. Still no batsmen lofted the ball during our time. Nor would the coaches pardon it," recalled Sharad.

It is easy to see where the seeds of Rahul's classical batsmanship were sown.

Sharad's passion for the game extended also to following it keenly on the radio. "We used to get up at 4 a.m. to catch up on the Ashes Series on Radio Australia. If cricket was played in England we would follow the sport on BBC Test Match Special which went into the late hours of the night," he recalled.

Sharad was also a good all-round sportsman. Besides cricket, he represented the university in hockey. He also dabbled in football as goalkeeper and in table tennis and badminton. His involvement in multi-games was to rub off on Rahul.

Sharad's playing serious cricket ceased as soon as he completed his graduation. "That was the best I could aspire for. After that it was simply a question of getting a job and pursuing a career," he said.

He completed his postgraduation in Food Technology with the Centre for Food Technology and Research Institute (CFTRI) in Mysore and then joined Noga, a food factory in Nagpur. Immediately after the Chinese aggression in 1962 he joined the Government of Sikkim's food company before making the decisive move to Bangalore.

In Bangalore he joined Kissan as assistant manager on 1 January, 1965. Those days it was a United Breweries company. It was sold to Hindustan Lever Limited only in the 1990s. Kissan, during that pre-liberalisation era, was a household name. It was big in fruit juices and jams, products that were to become Rahul's nicknames in the future. Meanwhile, Sharad's marriage with Pushpa was arranged by their families in 1967. Pushpa, at that time, was a lecturer in drawing and painting at a college in Indore.

After marriage the couple settled in Bangalore. Pushpa joined the prestigious University Vishweshwaraya College of Engineering (UVCE) in 1968. She served in the Architecture Department till 2001, teaching art-related subjects to the students of architecture. Over the years she held art exhibitions (of her paintings) all over the country, including select places like the Taj Art Gallery and Jahangir Art Gallery. In Bangalore itself she was inducted into the managing committee of the famous Chitrakala Parishat, Karnataka's show-cased deemed university of visual arts.

Pushpa, who during her student days tackled two courses, was just as motivated while pursuing her career as a professor at the engineering college. She started her quest for a doctorate in art, and to this end did her thesis on 'Professor Nicholas Roerich and his Himalayan Paintings'.

The research for this took her to art galleries all over the country and, after painstaking research for seven years, she was conferred her PhD in 1999 by the Bangalore University. Incidentally, she is the first from Karnataka to be conferred a PhD in art. Interestingly, the ceremony where she was awarded the doctorate caused a stir as all the television cameras and photographers focused on a young man busily clicking away with his camera and attempting to freeze for posterity the momentous PhD his mother was being given. That young man was Rahul Dravid, already a Test star and widely acknowledged as India's most accomplished batsman.

That day, at the PhD conferring ceremony, as the other awardees and audience clamoured after Rahul for his autograph, it was debatable as to who was more proud of the two: Rahul for his mother's splendid achievement or Pushpa for her son's exemplary success.

Chapter 3

Rahul Dravid: The Early Days

Indiranagar, where the Dravids live, is a decidedly up-market residential locality in Bangalore. It was not so in the 1970s and early 80s when the city did not extend beyond Ulsoor in the east. A few kilometers after the Ulsoor residential layout was the HAL Airport (one of Bangalore's Defence airports doubling up also for civilian flights), reckoned at that time to be outside the city limits. Indiranagar, wedged between Ulsoor and the airport, was looked upon only as an extension of Ulsoor. However, the excellent quality of the road that connected the city to the airport and passed beside Indiranagar attracted a lot of residents and corporates to seek property in the area. Gradually it became one of the most sought-after addresses in the city.

Thus the Indiranagar of today is a bustling beehive of activity. Residential bungalows, multi-storied flats and modern commercial complexes coexist cheek by jowl. Multinational software firms, glitzy shopping malls, trendy restaurants, pubs, bars, posh clubs and super specialty hospitals have mushroomed in what was previously an exclusive residential area.

Of course, when Rahul Dravid was in his pre-teens, most of these commercial activities were non-existent. There were very few bungalows or houses and the area was marked by a lot of huge vacant spaces. The Dravids themselves lived on the same street as erstwhile Test star EAS Prasanna, arguably one of the greatest off-spinners of all time, and Sadanand Vishwanath, undoubtedly one of India's most gifted wicketkeepers.

"Sadanand, in those days lived just two doors away. His younger brother Santosh Bhavani and I virtually grew up together and played a lot of cricket in the vast open spaces that dominated Indiranagar those days," Rahul recalled.

Most of the cricket the young boys in the locality played was confined to the tennis ball variety. Matches were staged against teams from other streets. "Occasionally we used to play cork ball cricket matches with the winners taking home pencils or small shields or such trophies. There were times when we used to roll out some small used coir mats on a near flat surface to try and play with cricket ball. Of course there was no pitch as such," he recounted with a smile.

Rahul himself was a short, skinny boy and saw cricket as just one more sport. "I loved team games. I was not particularly fascinated by cricket in the initial stages. In fact, I used to play a lot of hockey. The important thing though was that I enjoyed being with other young boys and hence looked forward to team sport in any form. Of course, a whole lot of kids in the area played cricket rather than anything else and I joined in the fun. The matches against the other teams in the neighbouring streets or locality brought forth a lot of competitiveness."

By today's standards, Rahul could be termed a late starter to formal cricket. These days, parents are keen to push six and seven-year olds into coaching camps. The young boys are forced into formal coaching with ambitious parents transporting them from house to camp, from camp to school and again from school to camp each day. Parents spend an enormous sum of money and time on these kids in the hope that they could vicariously live their lives through them.

For Rahul, though, things were very different. "I played just for fun those days. I became engrossed in the game a lot later. I had no formal coaching whatsoever till I was 13 years of age.

"My father used to play a bit of recreational badminton with PS Vishwanath—former Karnataka State Ranji Trophy player and a qualified Netaji Institute of Sport coach who went on to become a vice president of KSCA—and casually mentioned that I was keen on cricket. Those days KSCA used to run a summer coaching camp at the stadium for young boys. PS Vishwanath was in charge of the camp. The camp was already well under way when he asked my dad to bring me along."

It was then, at the age of 13, that Rahul took part in formal 'nets' and received coaching. He had joined the summer camp late that year. But now knew that there was this coaching camp to look forward to the next summer.

"Thus the following summer I enrolled in advance. PS Vishwanath, chief coach, who did the allocation of trainees to the various nets, sent me to Keki Tarapore (another former state player and NIS coach). From then on the KSCA system took over," said Rahul.

Rahul at School

Rahul's schooling was at St Anthony's till the third standard and from then on at the St Joseph's Boys School. Now St Joseph's is a big name for education in Bangalore. Some of the top names in various fields are Josephites. The St Joseph's Boys School and the St Joseph's Indian High School, both run by the Jesuits Society, have an impeccable reputation.

St Joseph's Boys School (SJBS), where Rahul studied, is situated on Museum Road. It shares a small ground on campus with St Joseph's Arts and Science College (SJA&SC). Both institutions have their own grounds elsewhere, SJBS at Mahatma Gandhi Road—a short distance away from Museum Road—and SJA&SC at the nearby St Joseph's Hostel, which it shares with SJCC, on Richmond Road.

Sabeer Bhatia, founder of Hotmail and the late Mark Mascarenhas of WorldTel were both products of SJBS. Sadanand Vishwanath too did his schooling till the 9th standard in SJBS. Thus when Rahul joined, he was simply walking in the footsteps of many an illustrious name of this outstanding institution.

"I played for both the juniors and seniors team at SJBS. But funnily cricket was not a major sport in school then. The inter-school cricket competition for ICSE schools was conducted by our rivals, Bishop Cotton School. So we were not too bothered about it. Our school hosted the inter-school hockey tournament. Thus hockey was a very big sport for us. Winning at hockey was everything," Rahul pointed out.

Luckily for Indian cricket though, the ICSE schools had a very structured format for sports. Unlike the majority of the schools which followed the SSLC (Secondary School Leaving Certificate) pattern and thus had their academic year from June to May, the ICSE schools had the calendar year as the academic year (they too have since fallen into the June-to-May pattern). The ICSE schools were just a handful in number, but this allowed them to plan and coordinate their curriculum better.

Thus there were set seasons for football, hockey and cricket. Cricket followed the football and hockey seasons. This was fortuitous for it allowed Rahul to also play cricket.

"I played four years of hockey for the school as centre half and later right half. We practised very hard as we wanted to win our own championship. We had a very good team. I played alongside Sandeep Somesh and Anil Aldrin (who represented India in two Olympics). I really enjoyed the concept of team sports and hockey was right up my alley," recalled Dravid.

It was around this time that cricket in SJBS got a shot in the arm with the presence of Fr Freddy Menezes, Sports Secretary, and Fr Dennis Coelho, the Principal. Fr Coelho had earlier served a stint as principal at St Joseph's Indian High School where cricket was a major sport. Test cricketers Syed Kirmani, Roger Binny, Raghuram Bhat, Sadanand Vishwanath, scores of state players including Jeshwanth, Abhiram and a whole lot of other cricketers had been educated in that school, and Fr Coelho thus was exposed to the game's demands and popularity.

"Fr Freddy was big on cricket. He was enthusiastically backed by Fr Coelho. They insisted that we could win the Cottonian Shield too. They decided that we would give it our best shot. This resulted in serious nets in cricket even during the hockey season," revealed Rahul.

Former Ranji Trophy player Najam Hussain was roped in as the coach. "He coached us for two years, followed by one year by Keki Tarapore. Suddenly, for me everything in cricket was falling into place. The summer camp (mid-March to May end) at KSCA was followed by daily evening nets at the school grounds from the start of the academic year in June. The school nets were different from the KSCA camp, for I now had the opportunity of playing with boys of my age. I started to really enjoy myself. Further, I was making a lot of runs in the Cottonian Shield and this further pepped me up."

By the time Rahul moved to the tenth standard, Tarapore had taken over as coach of SJBS. He was a former student himself and had had plenty of experience coaching youngsters. He coached SJIHS for the BT Ramiah Shield (for SSLC and HSC schools) and SJBS for the Cottonian Shield.

Tarapore was also closely associated with Bangalore United Cricket Club, one of the premier league teams of Karnataka. Tarapore used to be a sort of talent scout for BUCC and over the years he had roped in a number of talented youngsters to the team. Kirmani, Binny, Sadanand

Vishwanath, Raghuram Bhat, Abhiram, Carlton Saldanha, et al. were some of the players he had roped in for the club. The president of the club was Dr Captain K Thimmappaih who was also the president of KSCA. Thimmappaih had the distinction of scoring the maiden first class century for the state. He was vastly experienced as player, manager and administrator. He knew a good player when he saw one and was never shy of backing talent.

Tarapore, on whom Thimmappaih depended for recuiting youngsters to his club, recognising the talent in Rahul, asked him to join BUCC.

"He told me that I could come to nets whenever possible. Now this was great stuff for me. The club practised at KSCA in the morning and the school had its nets at the Webbs ground in the evening.

"Of course it was very tough for me. I lived in Indiranagar and from there went to KSCA in the morning for nets. Immediately after nets I used to rush to school (a couple of kilometers away). School, those days started at 8.30 a.m. In the evening, after school, I had to rush to the Webbs Ground (a couple of kilometers from the school) to be in time for the school nets. My parents were both working and it was very tough on them to get me ready in time each morning, pack my breakfast and lunch. They could not drop or pick me up and so it really meant ceaseless rushing from one place to another," revealed Rahul.

Tough as those early days were, they also brought a sort of regimentation and discipline in Rahul's schooling years. Of course, being an excellent student he had to devote attention on studies too.

"I was not very strong or big those days and this constant rushing about from one place to another for cricket nets and matches used to leave me exhausted. I think the fact that I found it enjoyable to be in a team sport kept me going. I was also getting a lot of runs and this goaded me into trying all the harder," said Rahul.

It was during his formative years and in school cricket that a challenge cropped up that would rear its head again and again right through his career: To keep or not to keep.

Chapter 4

Never Say *Never* Again

"How many wicketkeepers in this group?" Keki Tarapore, coach at KSCA's summer coaching camp, asked the young boys on the first day of the summer camp in 1986. The trainees, about 20 of them aged between 13 and 18 years, had come from different backgrounds, schools and localities. They, along with dozens others, had enrolled for KSCA's summer coaching programme.

Till the late 1980s, barring the Karnataka State Sports Council nets at Sree Kanteerava Stadium, there were few opportunities for youngsters whose school or club did not have a cricket coaching programme. This resulted in the Karnataka State Cricket Association's summer coaching programme being a big draw for youngsters.

The whole programme typically lasted 12 weeks. Each batch of trainees, though, underwent only four weeks training. There used to be a morning nets from 6 a.m. to 9 a.m. for one set of boys and another between 3.30 p.m. and 6 p.m. for the second batch. Training usually meant a bit of jogging, sprinting, stretching, some fielding practice, hanging-ball practice and a bit of batting and bowling. It was not a strenuous course as such, but gave the youngsters an insight into the game, its rules and intricacies. Later, the cream of the camps was chosen for an intensive but short training stint.

The best part of the whole exercise was that the young boys got to play every day of the summer camp at the hallowed KSCA Stadium. Of course, the initial net itself was at the KSCA matting facility which fell outside the main arena. But the jogging, stretching and fielding practice were sometimes in the main arena. And this stepping on to the hallowed turf on which Test matches and One Day Internationals were staged was in itself a big thrill for the young trainees.

Rahul, who had had his first taste of formal coaching at the previous summer camp when he joined towards the fag end of the programme, was not particular about what he wanted to do.

"I looked around. When Keki asked 'how many wicketkeepers in this group', not a single hand went up. I was just 13 years of age then. I said to myself, 'what the heck, let me give it a shot.' So I put up my hand. I had never kept till then. But I was willing to try anything at that stage.

"So I kept. And I actually enjoyed it. It kept me involved in the nets. And because there were no other wicketkeepers in that net, I got a lot of practice."

This proved to be a lucky break for Rahul. He was quickly identified as a wicketkeeper-cum-batsman. However, in his school junior team, he was not the wicketkeeper.

"We already had a wicketkeeper. It was only in my second year in juniors cricket that I kept wickets for the school. And even this because I was the captain!

"In fact I asked the boys if anybody wanted to keep. But nobody seemed prepared. So I donned the gloves."

The following year, when the St Joseph's Boys High School seniors team played in the Cottonian Shield, Rahul again did not keep wickets.

"I was not particular about wicketkeeping. There was already a senior boy keeping wickets. I was scoring a lot of runs and was happy letting somebody else do the job. But when I became the captain of the seniors team the next year, we once again did not have a wicketkeeper. So what do you do as captain?

"I grabbed the gloves and stood.

"The important thing though was that as a wicketkeeper, I had plenty to do in the nets. Otherwise just batting and hanging around would have been a big bore."

This extensive stint behind the stumps stood Rahul in good stead, for when the State Under-15 selection took place, he got into the Karnataka team as a wicketkeeper-cum-batsman. During Rahul's first year in the State Under-15 team, Sujith Somasundar (who later went on to open the batting for India in one-day internationals) was the captain. Karnataka played their opening match in Bangalore, against Andhra—and lost.

Rahul flopped with the bat, but impressed with his wicketkeeping. This helped him get into the South Zone Under-15 team as the second wicketkeeper. He went on be a part of the South Zone camp as wicketkeeper-batsman.

The following year Rahul scored a lot of runs in Under-15 cricket and also kept wickets pretty well. This got him into the South Zone side and ultimately won him a berth in the national camp in Calcutta. His batting was falling into place and he was constantly among the top run-getters. Wicketkeeping was a value addition but was getting him plenty of recognition. However, once again things were about to change for Rahul.

"It was my entry into college that shook me out of my comfort zone. In school I was top dog. I was wicketkeeping, I was batting, and I was whacking the ball all over the place, getting lots of runs and dominating the show. Suddenly, four months later, I was in a different league."

In school Rahul had things going his way. He was the captain, scored innumerable runs and generally did what he wanted. But all this changed when he joined St Joseph's College of Commerce. He was thrown into an ocean, or so it seemed.

"Here, I was, 15 years of age, competing not with boys my own age, but men, five to six years older. In the first year of college cricket I was dropped from the team. Of course I played for the PUC (pre-university college) team. But I was kept out of the main team. The captain, Satish Vishwanath, who had earlier played for State Juniors and was in the final year, was also a wicketkeeper. He would not let me play me in the team. A lot of the guys in the team had played State juniors and Under-19. I couldn't get a look-in. Besides there was a guy called Sanchit Menezes who had played with me in school. He was my senior and he too was a decent wicketkeeper. So I stopped keeping for college."

This apart, Rahul was no longer enjoying wicketkeeping. He broke a finger while keeping and this took the fun out of the job. It also laid him off the game for a few weeks. Besides, he had grown taller and all the squatting and getting up as a wicketkeeper was not helping him any. However, as a batsman Rahul was in the thick of action. He was scoring plenty of runs and seemed to be enjoying the role as pure batsman.

"Even in inter-club cricket I could not keep for my club, BUCC. The club already had Syed Kirmani and Sadanand Vishwanath competing for the wicketkeeper's spot. And if they were not around, NR Maaney, who was a decent former state juniors wicketkeeper, was the third choice wicketkeeper," explained Rahul.

There were few to challenge him when it came to batsmanship. Irrespective of whether he played for school, college or club, he would come in at number four and would score a lot of runs in style.

The added advantage for his teams to have Rahul in the side was that if the main wicketkeeper was injured or sick, or could not keep for whatever reason, Rahul would stand in and do a pretty efficient job.

Even as his role as a wicketkeeper seemed to be tapering off, Rahul, although he was just 16 years of age, was already batting like a champion. He broke into the state juniors side on the strength of his batting alone. The state juniors wicketkeeper that year was Avinash Vaidya, who was later to become a national wicketkeeping prospect. Then there was Gopalkrishna, another young promising keeper and Vinay Badami (son of former Test Umpire Satyaji Rao), who was also a good wicketkeeper-batsman.

"Thus I was not keeping regularly anywhere by now. The college team, the club team and the state juniors all had regular wicketkeepers and I was doing it just once in a way. And when you don't keep regularly, the sharpness goes, the momentum goes. So does the interest. So I told the selectors that I did not want to be considered as a batsman-wicketkeeper, but only as a batsman."

Rahul was just 16 then. But he was already sure that wicketkeeping was not his cup of tea. Fate, though, had its own plans for him.

Of course, Rahul never had to keep in Ranji Trophy matches. Karnataka had Kirmani and later Avinash Vaidya. Thus, nobody even spoke of wicketkeeping again to Rahul for the next seven years. He was scoring plenty of runs and had even started bowling before fate once again pushed him into wicketkeeping.

It started innocuously enough. Karnataka wicketkeeper Avinash Vaidya donned the gloves for South Zone in the national inter-zone Duleep Trophy tournament. It was the year 1995 and the main stars were busy with the home series against New Zealand. The series during October-November and also the Duleep Trophy that year, were run-ups to the Wills World Cup to be staged in India, Pakistan and Sri Lanka during February-March, 1996.

Rahul, like some of the other aspirants, was hoping to catch the national selectors' eye with some good performance in the Duleep Trophy. He had already slammed an unbeaten 145 for Board President's XI against the Kiwis before the start of the Duleep Trophy and knew that he was in with a very good chance.

Around this time, South Zone readied for their crucial game against West Zone at Alwar. It was then that Rahul was yet again forced to take to the big gloves.

"Avinash Vaidya injured himself on the morning of the match. Suddenly I was asked to keep. WV Raman was our South Zone skipper. I had not kept for seven years now and was naturally worried. Worse, the pitch was spinner-friendly and quite a bother. We had Sunil Joshi, Kanwaljit Singh, Anantha Padmanabhan and S Vasu in our ranks. All of them could be a handful on that track. But I took it as a challenge. We won the match and I must say I thought I kept well. We went on to win the Duleep Trophy that year and somebody mentioned my keeping," said Rahul.

That sowed the seeds for Rahul's greater stint with the gloves, for the following May, the main Indian team to tour England was selected. Nayan Mongia was the first choice wicketkeeper. In fact, he was the only wicketkeeper. The selectors opted for Sanjay Manjrekar to do the second wicketkeeper's job.

That tour to England was Rahul's first major tour with the Indian team. He had played in the Singapore and Sharjah tournaments just a few weeks earlier. But a Test tour was something else altogether.

Early on that tour, as fate would have it, Mongia suffered a finger injury and could not keep in some of the side games. Manjrekar stepped in, but lost interest after a couple of games. It was then that the team selection panel fell back on Rahul to keep in a few games.

"Yes, I was taken aback. But at that nascent stage of your career you are willing to do anything to get into the Indian playing eleven. I hadn't even carried a pair of gloves. I was that ill-prepared for the task. In fact, I was caught totally off guard. Anyway, I borrowed Nayan's gloves and tried to do my best.

"It was a bit of a challenge as the ball wobbled a lot in England. Also because it was so cold at that time of the year, you had to collect cleanly, failing which the ball would sting the palm despite the gloves.

And since I had had so little practice with the gloves, I was quite apprehensive. Luckily I did not keep in too many games!"

But if Rahul thought his foray into wicketkeeping on his first major tour was a one-off thing, he, and a lot of others, was in for a shock.

Again it was not something planned. Rahul, after that 1996 tour of England, hardly had another look at the gloves. As far as he was concerned, his wicketkeeping days were over (see also chapter 'The Glove Poser'). And so it was until the Sharjah tournament in April 1999.

The game was against the traditional rivals, Pakistan. Shockingly, five of the Indian players, Amay Khurasia, Ajit Agarkar, Nikhil Chopra, Vinod Kambli and wicketkeeper Nayan Mongia, were down with viral fever. While four of the players sat out the match, Mongia braved the fever and kept wickets as there was nobody else around. But try as he did, he could not continue beyond the initial 15 overs. Just as Skipper Mohammed Azharuddin was wondering at his plight, somebody recalled that Rahul had once been a wicketkeeper. It was then that Rahul was forced to pick up the gloves yet again. Though he had not kept wickets seriously for three years now, Rahul did a pretty competent job.

In the next match, against England, Mongia, standing up, was struck on the face by an Anil Kumble delivery and had to leave the field. Rahul, who had to do duty again, called for a helmet with a grill face-protector and stood for the rest of the match. He enjoyed himself so much in that match that he pulled off an excellent stumping to dismiss Graeme Hick off left arm spinner Sunil Joshi. Later, at a crucial stage in the match, he held a smart catch off Ajay Jadeja to terminate the dangerous Neil Fairborther's innings.

That Sharjah tournament was a disaster of sorts for Mongia. In the next match against Pakistan, another freak accident laid him low. Shahid Afridi, the well-built Pakistani opening batsman, crashed into Mongia while unsuccessfully trying to avoid getting run out. Mongia, however, injured his neck in the incident and went off the ground for quite a while. During that period Rahul took over behind the sticks and once again did pretty well.

Immediately after the Sharjah tournament came the 1999 World Cup in England. Once again, Mongia was designated the wicketkeeper. He did his duty in the first two matches against South Africa and

Zimbabwe, both of which India lost. The third match against Kenya threw up the twist that was to ultimately spell finish to his career.

India batted first and ran up a mammoth total of 329. Rahul, coming in at number three, scored a superb 104. Then, when it was the Kenyans turn to bat, Mongia injured his hand while failing to collect cleanly an express delivery from Javagal Srinath. The injury in the ninth over of the innings required attention. The team doctor, Dr Ravindra Chadda, bandaged the hand. This forced the team to fall back on Rahul to do duty as wicketkeeper too.

Rahul kept against Sri Lanka also before Mongia returned for the match against England. By now Rahul, without being spectacular or even brilliant, was seen as a decent wicketkeeper. He was keeping with the same competence as Mongia on the decline or his replacements, MSK Prasad, Sameer Dighe and Deep Dasgupta.

In fact, during the Aiwa Cup in Sri Lanka, Rahul replaced Prasad as the side's wicketkeeper. Likewise, later, in South Africa he displaced Dasgupta.

Of course, Rahul was not keeping wickets either for Karnataka or South Zone. This meant he was not getting sufficient match practice as a wicketkeeper. However, the Indian team constantly depended on him to either substitute behind the sticks or occasionally to take over as the main wicketkeeper.

Luckily for Rahul, this was happening only during major one-day tournaments and not in Tests. His wicketkeeping ability was seen as a big boon to the team, particularly as it sorely felt the absence of a good all-rounder.

Rahul's wicketkeeping was helping the team to have more options, particularly when it came to strengthening the batting line-up. Skipper Saurav Ganguly grabbed the opportunity and convinced him of the need to look at keeping in one-dayers as a means to strengthen the team. In any case, the wicketkeeping options available to the selectors were not so impressive that they could have done better than Rahul.

Thus, in the couple of years leading up to the World Cup in southern Africa in 2003, Rahul was already making his presence felt behind the stumps also. By the time the World Cup came along, he had done enough work as a wicketkeeper to inspire confidence in the selectors and his teammates.

Rahul kept wickets splendidly in the World Cup. His undisputed batting ability also lent an edge to the team and helped it perform better than it had since 1983. Thus, reluctant as he was, Rahul, right through his career, from school days to his stint at the highest level in international cricket, was pushed into wicketkeeping for the greater good and glory of his team. Having said never at the age of 16 and stayed away from this aspect of the game for all of seven years, Rahul's career as a wicketkeeper had come a full circle (see also chapter 'The Glove Poser').

Chapter 5

The Glove Poser

One memorable comment about wicketkeeping came from former India batsman TE Srinivasan.

TE, as he is popularly known, was member of the Indian team on the 1981 twin tour of Australia and New Zealand made famous by the near conceding of the Melbourne Test by Indian Skipper Sunil Gavaskar. So peeved was Gavaskar at being adjudged leg before wicket to Dennis Lillee that he very nearly succeeded in forcing fellow-opener Chetan Chauhan to walk off the field in protest.

The gregarious TE, who loves to talk and laugh a lot, made his foray into coaching at the end of his playing days. This was a tailor-made situation for him as it allowed him to pass as many witty and harmless comments as possible. In this he was as entertaining as he was while batting.

On one occasion, watching an India game, there was the unusual sight of erstwhile wicketkeeper Nayan Mongia calling for a helmet with protective face grill to stand up to leg spinner Anil Kumble. Those days, helmet and face grill were not standard wicketkeeping equipment. But with the tall Kumble, who bowls his variety of leg spin and googly at a brisk pace, getting the odd delivery to pop up and turn, Mongia, standing behind the wickets, opted for extra protection. It was then that TE made his unforgettable remark:

"Standing up to Kumble on these pitches pales into insignificance when compared to what Kiri (former India wicketkeeper Syed Kirmani) used to do. Those were the days we played Ranji Trophy and Duleep Trophy matches on some of the worst pitches. Teams used to get bundled out for 120 to 150 runs. Sometimes even these were winning scores!

"On such lousy pitches it was a nightmare batting against Chandra (BS Chandrashekar, India's legendary match-winning bowler who used to bowl his brand of leg spin, top spin and googly at a terrific pace). If one delivery shot through from a length at ankle height, the next one from the same length had to be fended off from the face. Batsmen with a bat in hand, pads and all sorts of protective equipment used to be petrified at playing Chandra on such pitches. But there was Kiri, standing up to the wickets and collecting the ball in all sorts of acrobatic style.

"Certainly he was the greatest ever wicketkeeper. But my own feeling is you had to be mad or absolutely brilliant to stand up to Chandra on such pitches without the benefit of these helmets. To this day I do not know whether Kiri was mad or brilliant. Why, even now when I think of batting against Chandra on such pitches I break into a sweat."

TE's observation comes to the fore when one takes into account the sad accident that spelt finish to the career of yet another Karnataka wicketkeeper. Sanjay Desai, who along with Roger Binny was involved in a then world record first-class opening wicket partnership, used to don the gloves whenever Kirmani was called away on national duty. Desai had played for Indian schools, Indian universities and was a regular member of the Karnataka team even when the stalwarts were available.

This Ranji Trophy match against Andhra was held in Manipal, a small university town near Mangalore. It was not a regular venue for first-class cricket. Although Chandrashekar and EAS Prasanna, along with GR Vishwanath, Brijesh Patel and Kirmani, were away in Australia with the Indian team, there was still left-arm spinner B Vijayakrishna to spearhead the Karnataka attack.

In that match, Vijayakrishna's 'chinaman' went through the last batsman's 'gate' and clipped the bails. Desai, standing up, was unsighted by the batsman. The flying bail struck him on the left eye and he permanently lost vision in that eye. Sanjay Desai, cut off in his prime by this unfortunate accident on the cricket field, never played the game again.

Wicketkeeping, by any yardstick, is a tough job. Anybody who has seen the battering Kirmani's hands and fingers have taken over the years will understand what a toll it takes of the purveyor of this trade. Kirmani's fingers, for instance, are all crooked now. Another Karnataka wicketkeeper of note, Sadanand Vishwanath too took a lot of punishment behind the sticks. Yet, in spite of all its hard work and bruises, a wicketkeeper's job is a thankless one. When he does a good job, few appreciate it, for it is his business to be efficient behind the sticks. But when he makes a small mistake, it is magnified and blown out of proportion. In an era when, with slow motion cameras and super slow motion replays, commentators dissect every fumble or perceived chance these mistakes are shown again and again until the wicketkeeper is made to look silly.

Did this make Rahul wary of wicketkeeping? That would be a difficult call to make. By nature he is extremely careful and guarded. He weighs the pros and cons in every situation before taking any decision or making a move. And again, before he makes a move he dwells on the minus points before committing himself. Alternately, he is not the one to flinch from a challenge. It is just that he is not impulsive. When he walks into a challenge he ensures he is thoroughly prepared and hence is seldom caught off-guard.

Rahul had kept wickets with some success in his early teens and at the junior level. He was clean and effective without being brilliant. It is possible that his childhood neighbour Sadanand Vishwanath and his brother Santosh Bhavani, both of whom were wicketkeepers, could have subconsciously prepared him mentally for wicketkeeping. However, it was his coach during the formative years, Keki Tarapore—incidentally, Sadanand's coach earlier—who introduced him to wicketkeeping. But as Dravid moved into his late teens he grew taller. Tarapore always nurtured a theory: tall players do not make good wicketkeepers. The fact that top-notch wicketkeepers Alan Knot, Syed Kirmani, Geoff Marsh, Wasim Bari, et al. were relatively short in height seemed to support his theory. Thus, as Rahul shot up to be a six-footer in his late teens, Tarapore had a hand in getting him to concentrate on his batting. However, since he had kept wickets constantly during his formative years, and in junior cricket, Rahul's movements behind the stumps were mostly correct, and effective. These movements were so ingrained in him that they came out instinctively whenever he kept wickets.

Rahul, though, was not keen on keeping wickets. Having shunned it at the age of 16 and not having kept for college, club and state, he just could not fathom how he would get to keep for India. On the eve of the 1997-98 season when Rahul was training at the KSCA stadium, I asked him one morning if he had ever thought of donning the gloves again, especially as he was forced to do a little bit of it on the England tour. Rahul looked horrified. I pressed that like Alec Stewart had for England, Rahul could bring a great deal of value addition to the team if he donned the gloves at least in one-day internationals. Rahul's reply revealed that he had already thought this one out in detail, weighed the pros and cons, and rejected it.

"I kept during my school days and in junior cricket. Keeping at the international level is a totally different kettle of fish. The pulls and pressures make it a full-time job," he said.

When I persisted and stated that the only problem would be to keep to Kumble for 10 overs, the quintessential Rahul came out with a matchless analysis of the difficulties.

"Actually keeping to Kumble would not be that stiff a problem. He is not a big spinner of the ball. It is the subtle variation of pace and spin and the bounce that I would have to cover. The problem would be keeping to Sri (Javagal Srinath). He gets tremendous movement off the seam, even with the new ball. The problem with keeping to Sri is that most of the time the tilt is into the right-hand batsman—the unnatural side for me as wicketkeeper. And the angle of the ball keeps widening. I have kept in the nets to him and found that the ball, after passing the batsman, keeps going away on the leg side. This, at his genuine pace, would not only test the wicketkeeper, but end up bruising the fingers of his left hand (the right-hand batsman's top hand). Unless a wicketkeeper can collect Sri's delivery cleanly all the time, he would end up with broken or bruised fingers."

Since those days, Rahul's value as a batsman has increased tremendously. On many an occasion he is reckoned as the team's number one batsman. And for him to flirt with a trade that exposes his precious left hand to probable injury would be suicidal.

Many purists have denounced the decision to make him keep wickets for the country. This includes Syed Kirmani, India's finest wicketkeeper to date. Kirmani, as the chairman of the national selectors has gone on record that he does not approve of Rahul keeping wickets.

"In my opinion India should unearth a specialist wicketkeeper who can bat a bit as soon as possible. The team management consisting of the skipper, vice-captain and coach and the national selectors have banked on Rahul to keep wickets in one-dayers. Of course the interests of the team come first. But sooner or later the interests of the team would be in ensuring that Rahul is in prime condition to bat at his best and a specialist wicketkeeper is left to do the job behind the stumps," said Kirmani. Of course, the arrival to the national scene of young Parthiv Patel and Ajay Ratra should ease the pressure on Rahul in the near future. Patel already looks like soon turning out into a top-notch wicketkeeper-cum-batsman. That certainly would be welcomed.

But what would always be the amazing aspect of Indian cricket would be how Rahul, who literally gave up wicketkeeping at the age of 16 and did not keep for college, club or state, was dragged into keeping for the country after a seven-year break. History would also show the irony of how, despite two of India's finest wicketkeepers, Kirmani and Kiran More, being in the five-man national selection committee and setting the agenda for team selection, the team's faith was placed on a reluctant wicketkeeper's ability to dig deep into his motivational powers and keep for the country at the highest level.

Rahul has already kept wickets at the World Cup level. There is nothing higher than that. It is one of the quirks of fate that try as he did to give up wicketkeeping, it was something that simply would not go away. When Rahul finally hangs up his boots—or should it be gloves—it would be interesting to see the impact wicketkeeping made on his overall career. Certainly his wicket-keeping saga would rank as one of the most peculiar cases in the history of the game.

Chapter 6

Tough Times Never Last, Tough People Do

'Child is the father of man,' wrote the poet William Wordsworth. The Rahul Dravid mould, likewise, was cast long before he evolved into the rock-solid 'wall'.

Sujith Somasundar, who opened the batting for India in a couple of one-day internationals against South Africa and Australia in 1996, played a lot of cricket at every level with Rahul. He was Rahul's captain in the Under-15, Under-17 and Under-19 Karnataka State teams. Rahul and he also made their first class debut in the same match, the Ranji Trophy knock-out tie against Maharashtra at Pune. Sujith, thus, is someone who grew alongside Rahul on the cricketing front.

Sujith vividly recalled the first time he saw Rahul: "I was already a regular trainee in this KSCA Summer Camp when suddenly in the middle of the camp a stylishly dressed boy in sparkling white clothes came to the nets. Even at that young age he had a presence.

"Actually it was very difficult to get into the KSCA Summer Camp. But here was this boy walking in mid-way through. I wondered, 'who the hell is this joining in the middle of the camp.' A little later I saw him pad up and bat. He was very, very stylish in his approach to batting. He made an impression immediately just with his style."

Within a couple of years Sujith stated that he knew Rahul was destined to play big cricket. "Those days he used to be very nervous. He used to have sweaty palms. I believe he was so nervous because he wanted to do really well. He was so unbelievably intense in his approach to the game even in those days."

The Summer Coaching Camp was just the introduction to formal cricket that Rahul needed. In no time he was sucked into the game.

"The KSCA system took over from then on. I just had to play and ensure that I did well," explained Rahul.

His career was given a big leg-up when he was selected into the St Joseph's Boys School Junior (Under-14) team that year. It sharpened his desire to excel and made him totally focused.

"We all played the game, no doubt," said Fazal Khaleel, who has been with Rahul right through, from kindergarten to the Karnataka Ranji Trophy team. They were classmates at St Anthony's Junior School and moved to St Joseph's Boys School together. From there they progressed to St Joseph's College of Commerce. Along the way they played the various age groups cricket together. Rahul, though, broke into the Ranji Trophy team six years before Fazal. They continue to remain close friends.

"Rahul was amazingly focused. He set goals for himself, spoke about it and went about achieving it with a determination that I have never seen. His commitment and involvement were always total, even in the young days. He could not understand how others could be anything but totally committed."

Reflecting on the early days in school cricket, Fazal drew attention to Rahul's passion and intensity for the game. "It was one of the first Cottonian Shield (Bishop Cotton School's Inter-school Under-14 cricket tournament for ICSE schools of Bangalore) matches we were playing. Because of rains our match was shifted from the junior ground to the main ground. It was a great honour for us. We were allowed to use the main pavilion on the first floor at Bishop Cotton's grounds and generally we all looked forward to the game.

"We took first strike. The openers had batted for a while before a couple of wickets fell. One of the openers was still batting when Rahul went in to bat at number four. Rahul played a glance to fine leg and took off for what seemed to be an easy single. But the non-striker would have none of it. He simply did not want to run. I remember Rahul had reached the non-striker's crease before being sent back. He hastily tried to return and was just a few inches short of the ground at the striker's end when run out.

"The non-striker's excuse was that he was too tired to run. Rahul burst into tears on the ground itself and kept wailing loudly throughout the day. He was inconsolable. He would be quiet. Suddenly he would remember the incident and wail all over again. And this went on throughout the day. He could not accept the waste of his wicket simply because the other batsman was too tired to run."

Over time those who played with him came to realise that for Rahul cricket was not just a game. He was desperate to do well and was mentally and physically conditioning himself to that end. Even at that young age he realised that any opportunity was not to be wasted. This was particularly true when it came to nets.

Rahul was perpetually driving himself ahead, both in sport and studies. But he had so compartmentalised himself that even at a young age he sought to gain maximum advantage from any situation.

He attended club or state junior nets in the morning and school nets in the evening. In between he was busy with his schooling and the activities associated with it. Thus he simply had no time to waste or goof off.

This was brought to the fore during cricket nets. Most batsmen used to bat seriously for a while before fooling around. But this was not the case with Rahul. If he batted even for 15 minutes he would ensure that he got the maximum out of it. Both Fazal and Sujith recall how he used to sharply talk to any bowler who fooled around while he was batting. Right at the beginning he would ask them where their imaginary fielders would be positioned and would bat to that. He would expect the bowlers too to bowl seriously and to their field.

"In many ways he was getting more out of nets than anybody else. It was not a put on. It was just that he was far too focused and serious than anybody else in the group. He brought this kind of focused play at nets at the junior level and to this day I have not seen him approach nets in any other fashion," said Fazal in open admiration of his friend from kindergarten days.

His hard work and intense play notwithstanding, Rahul had a streak of superstition that stayed with him. He was a great admirer of Sunil Gavaskar and GR Vishwanath. Early in his career he had read that Gavaskar always wore something new for every game. Rahul too decided that he would go with the idiosyncrasy.

"I don't think he could afford it at that stage," said Sujit. "But Rahul was a creature of habit. If he did something different on any day, and if coincidentally he also scored a lot of runs that day, Rahul would do that something every time he had a match.

"The first time he played with something new fetched him success. He became so superstitious that from then on he always wore a new item on a match day. It could be anything—a pin or socks or handkerchief, a shoelace, anything at all. But Rahul always wore something new before a match."

Apparently this 'wearing something new' was not the only fetish or superstition he had. Fazal spoke of a South Zone Under-15 Cricket Camp at Thiruvananthapuram, formerly Trivandrum, in Kerala.

"Some of us sat under a tree which was quite far from the pavilion. Rahul too was with us. He was padded and awaited his turn to bat in that camp match. When it came, he walked into the ground from that place under the tree. He went on to get a lot of runs in that innings. From then on, even if there was nobody under that tree Rahul would walk in to bat only from there. Sometimes he used to be alone under that tree, awaiting the fall of a wicket. He was so far away from the rest of us in the pavilion that it used to be funny. But Rahul was not bothered. His faith in his superstition was far greater than any fear of ridicule."

But even where superstition was concerned Rahul was far more intelligent than the others. He made sure that some of his superstitions worked for him by imbibing lessons that others missed out. Sujith who was Rahul's room-mate on many a tour pointed this out.

"Rahul always carried two books with him: *Tough Times Never Last, Tough People Do* by Robert Schuller and *The Power of Positive Thinking* by Norman Vincent Peale. He was very superstitious about these two books. Every night, before going to sleep he would lie in bed and compulsorily read a few pages from at least the Schuller book and then tuck it under his pillow before falling asleep. The Schuller book, in particular, was like a religion to him and over time he simply adopted that philosophy.

"I've read these books now and am aware of their message. But Rahul used to soak into this philosophy from the Under-15 days," said Sujith.

It is this kind of focus that Rahul brought into play, whether at camp or at nets, or in the matches, or even in his choice of superstition that channelled his energy into becoming a great cricketer.

Chapter 7

Finding His Feet in Junior Cricket

Rahul understood very early that junior cricket was only a stepping stone to bigger things. This might sound simple but it has to be understood that a great many youngsters' quest for a place in the state junior cricket teams was only to gain admission in engineering and medical colleges.

Of course, some realised pretty early that they were not cut out to play the game at the highest level and chose instead to seriously pursue a career in the sciences. In Karnataka, as indeed in a few other states in the country, representing the state in a major sport helped to gain admission to 'professional' colleges. Engineering and medical colleges in the state had a quota for sportsmen and getting into one of the many junior state teams (Under-13, Under-15, Under-17 and Under-19) was, for many, one of the easier ways to gain admission through the quota.

The admission into these courses was so intense that students usually needed marks in excess of 95 per cent to be considered for merit seats. The grace marks that went with sports quota thus came in handy in many situations. Indeed many a cricketer went through junior cricket with the sole aim of squeezing into these professional courses.

But this was not the case with Rahul. His ambitions in the game were far greater, as will be revealed throughout this book. On completion of his ICSE, he sat with his parents to decide his future. Rahul was very clear that he did not want to seek a career in either engineering or medicine as it would seriously curtail his pursuit of cricket.

"Rahul told us that he would opt for a course in commerce. If by chance he did not make it big in the game, he assured us that he would concentrate on a course in business management and get into the corporate world. We were in a position to asses his potential in the corporate world and knew that he could make it there even at a later stage. But since his interests and love lay in playing cricket we decided to back him to see how far he could go," said Sharad Dravid.

When still in school Rahul realised that the competition on the cricket field was immense and he needed to do everything possible to stay ahead of the pack. Once he came to terms with this he willingly went the extra mile right from a young age. The fact that he was very keen to do well and was not a shirker helped with the coaches and selectors. They saw talent backed by intelligence, sincerity and willingness to work hard, and therefore gave him all the encouragement.

In the process, Rahul also got a few good breaks. One was the absence of a wicketkeeper in his first camp at KSCA. He admitted that was the sole reason for him to volunteer to keep wickets. Of course, the fact that his neighbour was Sadanand Vishwanath, the Test wicket-keeper, must have subconsciously inspired him to try his hand at it. Whatever the reasons, his stint behind the wickets came in handy when he competed for a berth in the various age group teams. The selectors identified him as a wicketkeeper who could bat well. His wicketkeeping came as a value addition and thus gave him the edge in the early days.

In his very first year with the State Under-15 team, his wicketkeeping, rather than his batting, convinced the selectors to include him in the South Zone under-15 team. He went as a second wicketkeeper and later got into the South Zone camp.

"The selectors picked me for wicketkeeping. So in the strict sense it was my keeping that fetched me the break," said Rahul. That season, Karnataka played just one under-15 game, against Andhra in Bangalore, and lost. Rahul did not score many runs. Though his side lost, he still made it into the South Zone side as the second wicketkeeper. The boost was enough to fuel his ambitions further.

Rahul worked very hard at the Thiruvananthapuram camp and carried the hard work through the year. During this period he really put heart and soul into the school, club and state junior team nets.

In this Rahul was greatly helped by St Joseph's Boys School Principal Fr Dennis Coelho. Coelho was a strict disciplinarian for whom academics came first. In Rahul's case, though, he realised that the young boy was an outstanding student and whatever he missed by staying away from classes, he could easily grasp with a little bit of extra help. Coelho had confidence in Rahul's ability and motivation to catch up with the rest of the class in a very short time.

Fr Coelho's support was vital in his development at that critical stage of his youth. Without the support, Rahul could simply not have spent those crucial extra hours at the nets. Those days the state junior nets were at KSCA's matting facility. KSCA did not provide breakfast and such other facilities that now seem the norm for state teams' practice. Nor did the association then have a gymnasium, locker room and allied facilities.

Rahul would catch the early morning Bangalore Transport Service (BTS—public transport) bus from Indiranagar, his place of residence, to KSCA and work in the nets from 6.15 a.m. till 9 a.m. He would then change into school uniform on the deserted stairs of the Western Stand, for in those days there was no changing room facility in the outside practice ground. He would wolf down the breakfast he had brought from home on the same stairs and then, with cricket kit and school bag thrown over his shoulders, he would run the couple of kilometers distance to school.

Armed with his favourite fruit, apple, which he would devour while jogging to school, Rahul would reach late. On rare days he used to treat himself to a *masala dosa* at the now defunct Shreeraj Restaurant outside the KSCA. Often, by the time he made it to class a couple of periods would have lapsed. But since Rahul was an excellent student, Fr Coelho gave him special permission to come late to school. The teachers too did not mind.

"Rahul was a very fine person," recollected Fr Coelho, currently posted in Gulbarga, in North Karnataka. "I spoke to his teachers before giving him permission to miss a few classes. The teachers were unanimous in their praise for him and his academic abilities. They had no complaints at all about him. The sports secretary, who took a lot of interest in Rahul, too showered praise on him. It was then that I started to closely follow his development as an individual.

"Rahul had no conflict whatsoever with any teacher or student. It was not just exemplary; his relationship with fellow students and his teachers was ideal and flawless. It was unusual and, in a way, it was unreal," said Fr Coelho.

The fact that his principal backed him to the core was a great help. More so as he was allowed to skip the last period of the day also to attend nets in the evening. After nets he would once again wind his way back home on a crowded BTS bus. Effectively, he was home just for dinner and sleep.

All this slogging paid off when he made the State Under-15 team for the second year in a row. This time, the tournament was in Andhra and during the school term. The Dravids were hesitant whether St Joseph's Boys High School with its demands on academics would allow Rahul to miss classes to take part in a tournament in far away Vijayawada in Andhra Pradesh.

The Dravids—Sharad and Pushpa along with Rahul—met Fr. Coelho and apologetically stated that Rahul's cricket would interfere with his studies and therefore they could not ask Rahul to go to play in Andhra Pradesh.

In Fr Coelho's words, "I don't know if it is what I said. But much, much later, well after Rahul had become the excellent Test cricketer he is, they came to thank me and said that I had remarked: 'You leave studies to me. I'll handle that. You let him play cricket. It is a great adventure he is embarking on and let's support him'.

"I remember, though, that Rahul jumped with joy in my office when I gave him permission."

That year the South Zone Under-15 tournament was in Vijayawada. The Karnataka team had practised on matting wickets while the first match was to be played on turf. "We had never played a match on turf. In fact, I remember we were asking one another 'why do batsmen tap on the pitch during the match'," said Fazal Khaleel who led Karnataka Under-15 that year.

The unfamiliarity with turf pitches mattered little, for Rahul slammed a double hundred—his first big score in a representative game—Khaleel 150 and Karnataka made a huge first innings total.

"The only reporter at the ground was the *Indian Express* man in Vijayawada. We were very keen to see what was written about us and the innings we played. So next morning Rahul and I got up very early and walked out of the room at 6 a.m. in search of a newspaper. We got one after walking a lot and hurried back to the room. But before we could read the newspaper, one joker in our team spilt all the coffee on it. Both Rahul and I were very upset. Luckily the reporter concerned came to the ground with a copy of the newspaper and gave it to us later in the day," recalled Khaleel.

Although Rahul began the tournament very well, he failed in the next four innings. It was a rude initiation into the vicissitudes of form but served to prepare him for the highs and lows of his career.

Rahul, that year, made the South Zone team and subsequently the all-India camp at Kolkata.

An interesting episode that year related to the inter-zone tournament staged at Nagpur.

All the five zonal teams were staying at the MLA Hostel in Nagpur. The boys would rush to the ground floor to gulp glasses of the orange juice that Nagpur was famous for. One night after dinner when they headed for the orange juice, Rahul intensely studied another youngster awaiting his turn to get a glass of juice. The boy had a mop of curly hair on his head and looked sort of funny. Rahul drew Fazal's attention to the boy and said "Fuzz, in two to three years that boy will play for India."

"I looked at the boy who had this funny hair and then at Rahul and asked 'are you joking or what'," revealed Fazal.

"I had seen that West Zone boy bat. Yes, he played well but I could not see anything extraordinary that at 14 years of age somebody could predict he would play for India soon," said Fazal.

"Next day, when we poured through the newspapers, we found the boy had scored a big hundred for West Zone. 'Mark my words,' Rahul said again. I just laughed.

"In fact in less than two years that boy played for India. And the same day he was selected to the Indian team Rahul reminded me of what he had said that distant day in Nagpur," recalled Fazal. The boy, incidentally, was Sachin Tendulkar.

Chapter 8

The Quintessential Rahul Dravid

Rahul's interest in the game was fueled from a very young age by his father Sharad. Sharad, who had played university cricket when in Indore, had given up the game to concentrate on his career in Kissan, a company that was in the United Breweries stable those days.

Sharad gradually formed a club cricket team in Kissan which had players drawn from the UB Group companies. They had their nets at the St Joseph's Indian High School grounds, right opposite the UB beer distillery. The team figured in KSCA's state fifth division league. Sharad, on the strength of his being the president of the KSCA-affiliated Kissan Cricket Club, received complimentary passes for big matches staged at the KSCA Stadium. He took Rahul to all the Ranji Trophy matches from the time his son was just two years old.

"Over the years I took Rahul along with his friends in the locality and later my younger son Vijay. The other children used to lose interest in watching the games and be more excited by the snacks, soft drinks and food. But Rahul was glued to the game. He would want to know the name of each batsman, bowler and fielder and kept asking questions about the game. Slowly I realised that his interest in the game was much higher than the other children and I started taking only him to the various matches," said Sharad.

By the late 70s when Rahul could recognise cricketers on his own, he was sold on India's two erstwhile master batsmen, Sunil Gavaskar and GR Vishwanath. He used to ask his father to invite them home. Of course Sharad tried, without success. But he managed to get photographs of Gavaskar posing with Rahul and Vijay. This made Rahul a bigger fan of Gavaskar and his school of classical batting.

This apart, Sharad, through Rahul's formative years, kept drilling into him that his wicket was never to be gifted away. Another lesson that his father taught him was not to play strokes that would dismiss him. Thus with his then role model Gavaskar playing percentage cricket, his father drilling the same lessons into him at home and his coach Keki Tarapore feeding him more of the same at nets, Rahul was totally sold to the idea of wearing down the opposition.

Rahul's parents also laid down parameters for his continuing with the game. They insisted that he could play the game only as long as he did well in studies. A first class was the bare minimum they stressed.

"I told him that he should study when not playing. He should not while away the time. Also we kept telling him that whatever task he took up he should complete it. We encouraged him to play cricket but on the condition that his studies would never suffer," said Sharad.

These conditions had an amazing impact on Rahul. Blessed as he was with the ability to compartmentalise tasks, Rahul, like his mother, revelled in multitasking. His school friends speak in awe of his ability to study in a crowded bus each morning. There would be only standing room in the bus. Rahul would cling on to the vertical bar in the bus and read his school books unmindful of the din around him. He would get off the bus and straight away head for the nets. In the evening he would repeat this studying performance in the bus.

Rahul's ability to stay focused on whatever he had on hand won him great praise from his teachers. It is a trait that he took with success to the cricket ground too.

"I remember speaking to Sister Monica of St Anthony's School where Rahul did his primary schooling. Of all the students she recalled his involvement and commitment in everything he did even at that age. The teachers in my school too were all unanimous in giving him permission to play cricket. They all spoke of his focus and dedication. That impressed me," said Fr Coelho, his Principal at St Joseph's Boys High School.

Rahul's success at the Under-15 and Under-17 levels of interstate cricket brought him quick recognition. At the age of 16, he went on a private cricket tour to England. That tour was sponsored partly by Kingfisher (United Breweries). There were a number of talented youngsters on that tour. Besides, former Test player Roger Binny and state left-arm spinner Prakash Rathod, who were both in England at that time, played a few matches for the team.

On that tour, Sujith Somasundar was Rahul's room-mate. Sujith bowled a bit of medium pace and was a promising opening batsman. He got to play in quite a few matches and with a fair degree of success. Rahul, however, was yet to establish himself as a frontline batsman. He played in only a few matches and did not do too well.

With things not going well for Rahul on that tour, he became more intense and tried all the harder.

"Rahul used to be in a world of his own in England. We were two of the youngest in that team which had a good mix of youngsters, experienced league players and veterans. Rahul was so obsessed with the game that he would walk about and play imaginary shots all the time. Even when we were on the street or in any place other than a ground, Rahul would be thinking only about batting and play imaginary shots. In the night he would cry in the room as he recalled his being dropped from that day's playing eleven or failing with the bat. He wanted to get maximum out of the tour, but felt he was not getting anything," said Sujith.

This habit of Rahul's to play imaginary cricketing strokes had become something of a joke among his friends and family members. On one occasion, in Bangalore, he was en route from residence to airport to drop his cousin's father-in-law, S Viswam, a well-known Delhi journalist who had worked with *The Statesman* and *Deccan Herald*. Viswam, on reaching Delhi called up Rahul's father and told him that he had seen *cricket-natyam* being enacted at the airport that day!

Apparently, Rahul, while awaiting the departure call for Viswam's flight, was unmindful of the amused looks he was getting from others in the airport and went about playing his imaginary front foot defence, back foot defence, drives, cuts, pulls and sweep shots—movements that Viswam referred to as 'cricket-natyam' (a take-off on *Bharatnatyam*, a well-known form of Indian classical dance).

By the time Rahul moved to St Joseph's College of Commerce his obsession with cricket was matched only by his relentless studying habits. In a way he seemed to live a Jekyll and Hyde role. Most of the year, when he played cricket, his friends were the Fazal Khaleels and the Sujit Somasundars, boys who went through the KSCA cricket system with him. But off the field and closer to the annual examinations a different set of students were his companions—students for whom academic excellence was the only thing. Amazingly Rahul juggled with both aspects of his life superbly.

This remarkable ability to compartmentalise his quest for excellence in two different spheres was, perhaps, a talent he inherited from his mother Pushpa, who handled two postgraduation courses simultaneously during her student days and later pursued a doctorate in art and conducted numerous exhibitions even as she taught in an engineering college.

Indeed Rahul's academic excellence has seldom been talked or written about even as his cricketing acumen has received widespread attention. Father Eugene Lobo, his Principal at St Joseph's College of Commerce, currently with St Aloysius in Mangalore, spoke enthusiastically of Rahul's stay in the college.

"He was intellectually very good. All the teachers liked him a lot. Although we were a co-educational college with 30 to 35 per cent girls in each class, Rahul never allowed that to sidetrack him from his pursuit of academic or cricketing excellence," said Fr Lobo.

In fact, an interesting aside to this came from Fazal Khaleel: "We were studying in II PUC (pre-university college, equivalent of 12th standard) and had a class party at a friend's place. The whole class was coming to the party. We had also invited some other girls. It was the first party we were having with lots of girls around. Naturally we were all excited. Rahul badly wanted to come to the party. Now these were day parties, during class hours (when parents thought the students were at class rather than partying). But Rahul also had a BUCC (KSCA senior division league club team) game that day. He wanted to be at the party and we all tried to get him to skip the match. However, on the morning of the party he called me up and said he was going to play the match instead. He was so torn by the urge to be at the party and his love for cricket that he said he would catch up with me in the evening and wring all the details of the party out of me."

That year, Rahul stood second in the whole college in accountancy and third overall.

"Rahul's great gift was to absorb everything he read. He had time to read just once and he had to retain that in his mind," said Fr Walter

Anrade who returned as SJCC principal. Although Fr Anrade was not the principal during the five years Rahul was in SJCC, he was the principal before and after Rahul's stint in college. Anrade was very well liked by sportsmen in college, particularly cricketers as he went out of the way to prop them up. "I knew Rahul well. His parents had spoken to me before zeroing in on Commerce as his degree. I was very proud of him and spoke of him as a role model for the other students. He was very good in cricket, excellent in studies and very well-behaved. What more can any teacher ask?" queried Anrade.

Rahul helped the institution in many ways. When his Hindi teacher Amanula needed money for medical expenses, Rahul willingly contributed his mite.

"I never had to worry about Rahul. If he was not playing a cricket match he would be in class, rather than whiling away the time on Brigade Road or in the cycle stand," said Fr Lobo. Rahul, who was a Ranji Trophy player by the age of 17 and constantly on tour to play the various age group tournaments or Ranji Trophy or Duleep Trophy or India junior cricket, when not involved in intercollegiate or club tournaments, was seldom able to attend classes. But he was not one to take his studies lightly. He, therefore, depended on his teachers to give him some personal attention after class.

Two of his teachers, Mrs Lily David and Mrs Vaz, helped him a lot. The former, in particular, was a pillar of strength as Rahul and his dad openly acknowledge. TN Narasimha Rao, the Economics lecturer, was another who backed him.

Rahul used to go to Lily David's house in a bid to catch up with studies. She coached him and then set the agenda for his studies. She and Vaz always claimed that it was such a pleasure to teach Rahul as his grasping powers were above average.

GK Govinda Rao, the English lecturer, was another multifaceted personality who dabbled in theatre, films and union activities. He was very proud that Rahul did very well in life. "He had no airs. He was very polite, a gentleman to the core. In this he was unlike many other cricketers who put on airs after playing for just the college team. I cannot remember Rahul ever misusing his position or his achievements in college. He was very respectful, very cultured and very decent in a very serious way. Although he did not have the time to involve himself in the Students Union or in other extracurricular activities I can very well say that the Josephites are all very proud about the way he has carried himself to this day. His conduct has brought credit to himself, his family, institution and country," he asserted.

The amount of goodwill and praise that were heaped on Rahul by his school and college teachers and classmates was simply staggering. Nobody had a single jarring word to say about him. It is unlikely that any other sportsman in India has achieved as much as he has and still conducted himself in such an exemplary manner.

"I made it a point to keep the TV room open even during class hours wherever Rahul was batting in Tests or One-Day Internationals simply because I feel that the values he stands for will be a shining example for young students. I know he will never be satisfied with mediocrity in anything he does. If the students want to watch him play and in the process imbibe even a small percentage of his values I know my role of an educator will be complete," stressed Fr Anrade.

Considering that the Josephites have had scores of international sportsmen in every discipline and have taken a lot of pride in their achievers in other fields too, the pedestal on which they have put Rahul is a pretty lofty one.

Chapter 9

Things Fall in Place

Rahul's days as a wicketkeeper seemed to be over when he stepped out of school cricket and into college cricket. He was not a regular wicketkeeper for college, club or even the state juniors, and therefore seemed to have reached a dead end as far as that aspect of the game was concerned. But just as one door was being shut in his face, another was slowly opening up.

It started innocuously enough. Rahul, at 16, told the selectors he was no longer interested in keeping wickets. This led to him not keeping wickets in the nets either. Before this typical nets for Rahul meant some physical training, fielding practice with him as wicketkeeper collecting the throws from the fielders, batting at the nets and a lot of wicketkeeping. This regimen ensured that he stayed involved in the nets most of the time—when he was not batting he was keeping wickets, and vice versa.

But once he gave up wicketkeeping, Rahul had plenty of time in his hands. "I hated the system of finishing batting and then hanging around in the nets. I was very uncomfortable with it. I simply had to do something or the other. So I did what seemed very natural—finished batting, picked up a ball and started bowling right through the nets session," said Rahul.

Rahul reasoned that he had neither the physique nor the rhythm to be a fast bowler. So he experimented with off spin. The best part of this is he started doing it pretty effectively. This opened an entire new range of options for him and his team.

He enjoyed bowling and soon started to bowl for Karnataka at the under-17 and under-19 levels. It began with a few overs, and soon he was turning his arm over pretty regularly. Of course, with all the runs that he was scoring, he was still being considered as a batsman, but his off-spin bowling was opening a few avenues.

It came to the fore when a young New Zealand team toured India. The Indians fielded an under-19 outfit but the Kiwis did not restrict themselves to any age group and had a lot of older boys in the team. This enabled them to come up with an excellent New Zealand team which provided very good competition on the field. But off it they constantly cribbed about India and the facilities provided at many of the centres.

The visitors had Stephen Fleming, Dion Nash, Mathew Hart, his brother Robbie Hart, Jeff Wilson—who went on to become an All Black star—and a whole lot of others. They played a lot of good cricket on the tour. They lost one Test by mere 12 runs and went down in the one-dayers by a 2-1 margin.

Rahul, who led the India Under-19 team in that series, did well with the bat. But it was as an off-spinner that he sprung a surprise. He bowled a few overs in the second Test and then followed it up with some superb spells in the three one-dayers. His bowling analyses in the three matches speak for themselves: 10-0-28-3; 10-1-27-1; 10-0-34-1.

Rahul was not a big spinner of the ball, but was spot on target. He brought variations in flight, trajectory and pace into play and was by all means a pretty effective bowler. Unfortunately though, Karnataka, for whom he played in the Ranji Trophy, had far too many frontline bowlers—Javagal Srinath, Venkatesh Prasad, David Johnson, Dodda Ganesh, Mansoor Ali Khan, Raghuram Bhat, Anil Kumble, Sunil Joshi, K Jeshwanth and R Ananth—right from the time Rahul came into the side. Of course, all of them did not play together. However, any four in any combination was still a pretty potent bowling attack and by the time they were through most sides were dismissed. Rahul, therefore had very few opportunities in bowling at the first-class level. And unless a bowler sends down at least 500 overs in all forms of the game each season, he would not have sufficiently honed his skill.

It is possible that Rahul might have become a top all-rounder if he had turned out for some other state where his bowling prowess would have been allowed to develop. But playing for Karnataka that aspect of his game was never allowed to flower.

Interestingly, Rahul had the temperament to be a good bowler. Rajesh Kamath, former state player and assistant coach at the National Cricket Academy, revealed how Rahul had bowled in a league encounter between HAL and Syndicate Bank. Those days, when still in college, Rahul turned out as a guest player for HAL in the banks and industries league. Syndicate Bank had a number of first class players in Sudhakar Rao, AV Jayaprakash, Ramesh Rao, Rajesh Kamath, Shavir Tarapore and Sanath Kumar.

In Kamath's words, "The scores were tied. HAL had made 185 and we were 185 for six when Rahul started the last over. Okay, we took it easy. But suddenly in one over, without adding a run, we lost all the remaining four wickets. Two batsmen were run out and two others got out to Rahul and the pressure. Right through that over Rahul kept his cool and bowled on the spot."

Perhaps if there had been a lot of international cricket for juniors those days, then Rahul might have got an opportunity to develop as a bowler.

Instead he played just that one series against New Zealand as an under-19 cricketer. "These days, youngsters have so many opportunities at the under-15 and under-19 level. There's the Asia Cup, World Cup and also reciprocal tours. We had nothing of this sort. The only international under-19 cricket I played was when I was virtually a few months short of my 19th birthday," he said.

That India Under-19 team had a number of promising youngsters. Tamil Nadu's S Sharath, for one, scored lots of runs in all levels of the game, yet was never given a chance to represent India at the highest level. He simply could not get past his own state selectors. Then there were Tanveer Jabbar, another fine player, Akash Malhotra, Amit Pathak, Gautam Vadera, Abhijit Kale, Gautam Dutta, Suresh Kumar, et al. Yet from that India Under-19 squad only Rahul went on to play Test cricket.

"I think if there had been more under-19 tours a few from that crop would have played Tests," offered Rahul. "Many of them were good but lacked opportunities to further develop their skills."

Rahul's stint with India A was just as satisfying for him. He played a lot more cricket at this level, with the toughest one being against England A in India. England had a very good mix of players who had already made it to the international level and some extremely promising ones. All had played first-class cricket and were therefore quite seasoned compared to the India A players.

Leading the pack of experienced players was Mark Ramprakash, Skipper Allan Wells and Ian Salibury. They also had a number of fine players in Michael Vaughan, Nick Knight, Damien Cork and Richard Stemp. Besides, Min Patel, who was to grow close to Rahul when the latter spent a season with Kent, was also a member of the team.

The Indian side had some excellent youngsters in Rahul, Saurav Ganguly, Vikram Rathore, Vijay Yadav, Rajesh Chauhan, Sairaj Bahutule, Paras Mhambrey, Abey Kuruvilla and Amol Majumdar. The captain was former Test batsman Praveen Amre.

It was a good series between a strong side and a talented, but young, team. England, riding on the strength of their batting, won the Tests 3-0 and the one-dayers 2-1. Rahul himself had a good series, notching up four half-centuries. He made 47 in one innings and on another occasion, at the Eden Garden, he was batting on 25 when his partner Saurav Ganguly ran him out.

Rahul had played the ball to deep mid-on and came down the track for what would have been a simple single. But Ganguly, even as the ball went past him, turned his back on Rahul. Both were in the same crease and with Ganguly refusing to budge Rahul tried to unsuccessfully scamper back to the striker's end. It was only one more of the run outs involving Ganguly.

Just before this series, Rahul had gone with the India A team to Dhaka for the Saarc cricket tournament. The Indian team got the better of all the other Saarc cricket-playing nations, Pakistan, Sri Lanka and Bangladesh. It was a particularly low-scoring tournament on pitches that decidedly favoured bowlers. The highest total before the final was Bangladesh's 172 in their one-run win over India. Pakistan, for instance, was shot out for 120 in 47 overs by India. In another match, India defended a low total of 182 against a Sri Lankan batting line-up that had Marvan Attapattu, Hathurasinghe, Samarasekara, Russel Arnold, Indika de Saram and Upal Chandana and won by 44 runs.

The Indian team had Rathore, J Arun Kumar, Amre, Ganguly, Atul Bedade in the top order. But it was Rahul's batsmanship with scores of 44, 16, 33 and 37 that clinched the issue for India. On pitches that the others in the side struggled, Rahul put his head down and grafted for these small but crucial scores to pilot India to a triumph.

His performance in that low-scoring series proved that he was the man of the hour when it came to batting in crunch situations. And so it has been right through his career.

At that time, the national selectors took note of Rahul's performance in the two India A tournaments, in Dhaka and at home against England A. The following year, even as Rahul failed to make the Indian World Cup team, the selectors chose him for the India A's challenge in the Interface Cup in Sharjah.

Once again Rahul underscored his potential with some sparkling batting and cool temperament. His unbeaten 69 which helped India squeeze out a thrilling penultimate ball win over Pakistan was the high point of the series. Rahul with scores of 40, 69 n.o, 63 and 45 n.o. bagged the 'man of the series' award. India beat traditional rivals Pakistan by seven wickets in the final to make it doubly sweet for Rahul.

Things, thus, were falling in place for Rahul. He had made lots of runs at the Ranji Trophy and Duleep Trophy levels, was seen as a success at the India A level and had even smashed an unbeaten 145 for Board President's XI against the visiting New Zealand team. It just required the selectors to see that this 22 year-old was indeed the batsman they were looking for to shore up the national Test line-up.

Chapter 10

Making the 'Wall' of Fame

Long before Rahul earned the sobriquet 'The Wall', he had a coach who helped to lay the foundation for his solid play.

In his pre-teens Rahul had no formal coaching as such. His father Sharad passed on the odd tip or so. Most of the early cricket he learnt was through discussions with classmates and neighbourhood friends, including Santosh Bhavani, brother of Sadanand Vishwanath. The garage door served as their wicket and all the cricketing lessons about firm top hand, loose bottom hand, playing close to the body, etc. were learnt on the streets of Indiranagar.

Rahul was close to 13 years of age when he attended his first formal camp at the KSCA stadium. PS Vishwanath, former Karnataka batsman and vice-president of KSCA, was looking after the KSCA nets at that time. He remembered Rahul's father Sharad, with whom he played recreational badminton, telling him of his son's interest in cricket.

"I asked him to send Rahul to the KSCA camp. Those days there was very little coaching for young boys. I used to be the director of the Regional Coaching Camp at Sree Kanteerava Stadium. We had three-month long camps throughout the year for all games, not just cricket. Suddenly the state government decided to bring this under the Directorate of Youth Services and Sports. The coaches all became government officers and the camp just died.

"It was then that I requested C Nagaraj, erstwhile secretary of KSCA, to start at least a summer cricket camp at KSCA."

Those days, KSCA conducted nets and camps only for boys selected in state teams, and even that only during the season. It was left to the private clubs to spot youngsters at inter-school level and take a hand in their development.

"There was no direct contact between KSCA and the hundreds and thousands of children who wanted to play the game. Besides there were no private coaching camps like the ones that have sprouted all over these days," said Vishwanath.

The summer coaching camp was KSCA's way of direct contact with the young aspiring players. Initially, KSCA club members' children were inducted into these camps. They brought along their friends and relatives and the camp soon grew into unmanageable proportions. It reached a stage where KSCA had to conduct selections to choose trainees for the camp.

In this scenario, when Rahul walked into the camp, Vishwanath directed him to Keki Tarapore's net.

Tarapore was an off-spinner. He had played for the then Mysore State in Ranji Trophy against erstwhile Madras in 1945. He was a member of Bangalore United Cricket Club (BUCC), one of the more influential clubs in the state. Capt K Thimmappiah, who had the distinction of scoring the first Ranji Trophy century for Mysore State, was the president of the club. He was also the KSCA president, a post he took over from M Chinnaswamy.

Thimmappiah had a monopoly on selection committees. He was in all selection committees, whether it was to select the state schools side or the Ranji Trophy team. He had an eye for talent and was not shy of airing his views. Thimmappiah and Tarapore had a good rapport. The latter would be on the lookout for talented youngsters and alert Thimmappiah whenever he came across any.

Tarapore took to coaching and underwent the Rajkumari Sports Coaching Scheme in Bombay in the late 50s. He served a brief stint in Jaipur before being transferred to Bangalore. There, he was on deputation to the erstwhile Mysore State Cricket Association.

In Bangalore, for the next three decades Tarapore literally breathed cricket. Being a Parsi, he could stay at the Parsi apartments, just a stone's throw from the cricket stadium. He was at the association grounds early in the morning for the nets. Later he would travel in his moped or scooter from ground to ground to watch his wards play either inter-school or inter-club or any match, for that matter. In the late afternoon he was back at the club or state association nets.

Cricket, for Tarapore, was everything. Over the years, a number of Test cricketers ranging from VV Subramanyam, EAS Prasanna, BS Chandrasekhar, GR Vishwanath, Brijesh Patel, Syed Kirmani, Roger Binny, Raghuram Bhat and Sadanand Vishwanath attended his nets.

(Tarapore's son Shavir too played a bit of cricket before venturing to cricket umpiring. He is in the national panel and has stood competently in a number of one-day internationals.)

In the late 70s and 80s, long before the advent of the National Cricket Academy, the Board used to run a national camp for promising youngsters. Former Test cricketers Col Hemu Adhikari and later Hanumath Singh used to be the chief coach and Tarapore assisted them. A number of outstanding cricketers like Kapil Dev, Yograj Singh, Bharath Reddy, B Arun, K Srikanth, Ravi Shastri, Kiran More, Sadanand Vishwanath, Raghuram Bhat, Shivlal Yadav, Roger Binny, et al. were put through their paces by Tarapore.

While Tarapore certainly had a big hand in the moulding of Roger Binny, Raghuram Bhat and Sadanand Vishwanath in the Karnataka line-up, the one cricketer he groomed from scratch was without doubt Rahul Dravid.

Coach and pupil struck an excellent rapport right from the start. For Tarapore, Rahul was everything he wanted in a pupil, and for Rahul, Tarapore's word was the gospel.

Rahul trusted Tarapore totally. His implicit faith in him was so strong that he accepted without question his instructions.

"Keki (Tarapore) moulded him. I can say this without doubt," said Sharad Dravid.

He had such tremendous interest in Rahul's cricket that he often set up special nets for him. Tarapore, who was a good communicator with youngsters, ingrained in Rahul the ethics of the game. By default, it also became the ethics of his life.

Rahul, in his teens, grasped these lessons quickly. Along with the values his parents, school and college teachers taught him, and the literature he was getting exposed to, he was turning out to be an upright, principled and very fine sportsman. In fact, these traits are unmistakable in him and anybody who has come in contact with Rahul over a period of time will easily vouch for it.

While Tarapore certainly was the coach for Rahul, he was also getting inputs from others. At the Brijesh Patel Cricket Academy he was exposed to the experiences and observations of former cricketers GR Vishwanath, Ashok Mankad, Roger Binny, Daljit Singh and Patel himself.

Daljit and Binny were perhaps the first to drive home the need to have a lot of stamina and be physically fit. Otherwise, most physical training involved a few laps around the ground, a couple of sprints and a few loosening up exercises. The Indian cricketers of the 1970s and 80s did not take physical conditioning seriously. Some of the biggest names in Indian cricket scoffed at the need for physical training and even ridiculed it during that period. One said that he got all his exercise while running between the wickets while another went on record to say that all the physical training he needed was got when he played shuttle badminton once a week!

Luckily for the aspiring cricketers from Karnataka, Daljit and Binny, during the later stages of his career, were exposed to developments elsewhere and imbibed the need for rigorous physical training. An entire generation of impressionable youngsters of that period, including Javagal Srinath, Venkatesh Prasad, Anil Kumble and Rahul, learnt their lessons well and took physical training very seriously.

Thus with the physical training, his inborn mental toughness shored up by the books on mind games that he read and his supreme commitment to practice, Rahul, as a cricketer developed rapidly. The best part of his early career was that he had an open mind about everything. He was a keen listener who assessed the pros and cons and then went about taking his own decision. Rahul has these traits even now. To this day he does not flinch from approaching ex-cricketers and asking them about their experiences, may be on a bouncy track, or on conditions where the ball seams.

This constant desire to improve and excel has seen him seek a batting tip or two from stalwarts like Sunil Gavaskar, GR Vishwanath and Ravi Shastri. "At the end of the day I think destiny lies in your own hands. If somebody who has been through it can provide insights into what you are walking into, you can be that much better prepared," said Rahul.

When he learned that the bounce of the South African pitches would be higher than in any he had played till then, he decided to prepare for it. He used the paved pavilion steps at KSCA Stadium as the pitch and got a few of his Karnataka teammates to wet a tennis ball and throw it at a short of length from 10 to 12 yards. He sometimes used a bat to defend and on other occasions discarded the bat and just concentrated on swaying out of harm's way. In the nets he made some of the fast bowlers bowl at him from 18 to 20 yards.

Of course, a lot has been said and written about how Sachin Tendulkar prepared for Shane Warne in 1998 by scuffing the pitch in the nets and getting local leg spinners to bowl in the rough. Very few, though, know that Rahul had prepared just as diligently to take on the South African pacemen, Allan Donald, Brian McMillian, Shaun Pollock, Fanie de Villiers and Lance Klusner, in their backyard during the 1997 series. The 148—his first Test century—and 81 he scored in the two innings at the Wanderers Stadium in Johannesburg is proof that all the hard work paid off. In fact, Rahul had such a splendid series that he was often seen as the side's number one batsman, ahead of Tendulkar and Mohammed Azharuddin.

Rahul's batting, though, was diametrically opposite to Tendulkar's. The latter sought to stamp his authority by dominating the bowling. Rahul took a different route. His aim was to frustrate the bowler by wearing him down. In this, his monumental patience and belief in his ability to stonewall helped. He presented a dead bat at most times and then every now and then came up with a stroke of exquisite timing to frustrate the bowler.

The pull, hook and cut which he grew up with on the matting wickets of Bangalore always stood him in good stead, particularly as he was not a compulsive hooker. He would sway out of the way often and then suddenly come up with a rasping shot to peg back the bowler.

"We used to call him the 'Rock of Gibraltor' even at that young age," said coach PS Vishwanath. "Keki and I knew that as long as he was there he would keep one end going. To this day that is the way he plays the game. Others like Tendulkar, Laxman and Ganguly get the confidence to play an attacking game when he is holding the other end rock-steady."

PS Vishwanath stated that he and Keki advised Rahul to give up wicketkeeping and concentrate only on batting. "It is too strenuous—keeping the whole day and then going out to bat at number three. Even now I hold that he must give up keeping. Wicketkeeping for a short while in one-dayers is one thing. But if he keeps in games of longer duration his batting will suffer."

Rahul took Tarapore's advice seriously. Of course, not being the number one wicketkeeper for college, club or state juniors also helped him arrive quicker at the decision. The point, though, is that Tarapore had a great influence in Rahul's line of thinking. This continued till Tarapore passed away a couple of years ago.

Rahul never forgot what Tarapore did for him in the early stages of his career. He made it a point to meet him before embarking on any tour, series or major match and also met him on his return each time. Tarapore, who used to go from ground to ground to watch Rahul play, took to following his career through live telecasts. If he thought Rahul was doing something differently or some error had crept into his basics he would note it down and alert Rahul about it.

Of course, in the later stages the talk might not always have been of cricket, but the bonding between the two was excellent. When Tarapore fell sick and ultimately became bedridden, Rahul organised a benefit match for him.

In subsequent years the advent of the e-Cricket Pro tool, the software the Indian team uses, helped Rahul analyse his game and that of his opponents. He took to the gizmo enthusiastically and this further fortified the already impenetrable wall.

For Rahul his career has been one long learning phase. At no time has he believed he is the master of the game. Yes, he has had that quiet confidence about him. But it is a confidence that comes cloaked with humility and a desire for perfection. In this he shows the same hunger to learn and imbibe that he did 17 years ago. It is this trait that has helped him become one of the finest batsmen in the world.

Chapter 11

Rising to the Occasion

Young Rahul's career was progressing very well. He had played at the under-15 and under-17 levels with a great deal of success. He also broke into the under-19 ranks while still just 16 years of age. But the real boost he got to his career was when he was chosen for the Karnataka Ranji Trophy team. And behind that selection lies a tale.

Karnataka, for years, was splendidly served by EAS Prasanna, BS Chandrashekar, GR Vishwanath, Brijesh Patel, Sudhakar Rao, Roger Binny, Syed Kirmani, AV Jayaprakash, Vijayakrishna and Sadanand Vishwanath. The retirement of Prasanna and Chandrashekar, followed soon by all the others barring Kirmani created a sudden vacuum in the team. Binny opted to play as a professional for Goa while Sadanand was dropped. The replacements for these stars were very weak. Opener Carlton Saldanha and all-rounder Karthik Jeshwanth were doing a good job while the left-handed batsman Arjun Raja was at last blossoming into a good player. Of course, left-arm spinner Raghuram Bhat was still getting amongst the wickets, but his body had taken its toll after all the bowling. Off-spinner R Ananth was also improving by the day.

Three promising youngsters, Anil Kumble (who had made his debut in 1989-90 and had played one Test in 1990), Javagal Srinath and Venkatesh Prasad, had been drafted into the team. Kirmani, the captain, was the most experienced member of the side.

In the meantime, on the administration front the old selectors had all quit and GR Vishwanath, Patel and Sudhakar Rao joined BS Chandrashekar as the state senior selectors. They coaxed KSCA to conduct the SA Srinivasan Trophy (KSCA's annual cricket tournament to help spot talent) on a league basis. Accordingly, the ten teams from all over Karnataka—Mysore Zone, Dharwad Zone, Raichur Zone, Mangalore Zone, Tumkur Zone, various Bangalore teams, et al.—were divided into two groups of five teams each. One set of league matches was played in Mysore and the other in Bangalore. The selectors, all experienced former cricketers, went around and watched the matches. They had already made a number of good inclusions into the Karnataka Ranji Trophy team (Kumble, Srinath, Prasad) and were looking to further shore up the side.

Karnataka during that 1990-91 season made the knock-out phase of the Ranji Trophy. The then format for the tournament was the various state teams would play in their respective geographical zone—East, West, North, South and Central—on a league basis and the top two from each zone would qualify for the next stage which would be on a knock-out basis. Karnataka and Hyderabad qualified from the South. Nevertheless, the Karnataka selectors felt the batting was not strong enough and wanted to strengthen it.

Usually, selectors go for experience in the knock-out phase, especially as the best of the teams including Mumbai and Delhi would have made the grade. Experience and ability to handle pressure would be a great source of help at this stage of the tournament.

"Our thinking on this was slightly different," reasoned Patel. "When you are young, you have youth and arrogance on your side. You are not too bothered about reputations. In fact, you take it as a challenge and try to pull down a few stars. If youth and arrogance are backed by a lot of ability and self-confidence a batsman would generally come good. The trick is in spotting the right guys. Also this works well with batsmen, rather than bowlers."

The selectors had already decided among themselves that Rahul and Sujith Somasundar would get the nod if they did well in the Under-19 tournament. In that tournament, Karnataka were in the knock-out and were playing Uttar Pradesh at Ahmedabad. Both Rahul and Sujith scored centuries in that match. That same evening they got the call from the selectors and were asked to rush to Pune.

Rahul, at 17, was over the moon at the news. Not too many at that age get a shot at first-class cricket. Here he and Sujith were being asked to join the team for a knock-out game against a strong Maharashtra team. Both rushed to Pune via Mumbai. By the time they reached Pune, it was very late in the night. They spent the night at Rahul's uncle's house and joined the team at the ground the next morning.

Rahul was not slated to be in the playing eleven. But in the last minute he was included. The Nehru Stadium pitch those days was likened to a billiards table top. It was supposed to be a batsman's paradise. Maharashtra, with experienced first-class cricketers Surendra Bhave, Milind Gunjal, Shantanu Sugwekar, Jedhe, More, Jadhav, et al., was considered to be a very strong team. On their home soil they expected to get the better of a Karnataka team filled with unknown youngsters.

In fact, some of the Karnataka team members did not know each other too well. Srinath, himself a fresher in the team, hailed from Mysore. He casually asked Rahul where his father worked. When Rahul stated 'Kissan', he said: "Oh! That juice-jam company." From then on he started calling him 'juice-jam'. The nickname stuck, though the 'juice' part of it was dropped somewhere along the line. The rest of the team members too started calling him 'Jam' and sometimes 'Jammy'.

The Ranji Trophy knock-out match went as per script for the Maharashtra team as they reduced Karnataka to 200 for five. On the flat Nehru Stadium track even 500 would not have been sufficient against the strong home team batting line-up. It was at this stage that debutant Rahul walked out to join Jeshwanth. The latter was in ominous touch that season. He had scored a huge double hundred against Tamil Nadu in the league phase and needed some sort of support at the other end to carry the team to safe waters.

The 17-year-old Rahul proved the ideal foil. He batted with remarkable poise for one so young and inexperienced. Rahul made 82 and Jeshwanth 175, and the sixth wicket pair added a whopping 238 runs. Karnataka made a massive first innings total of 638.

Rahul certainly made a very good impression in that debut match. But the man who stole the thunder in that encounter and made the national selectors sit up and take note of his fiery pace was a tall, skinny fast bowler who went by the name Javagal Srinath.

On that flat bed of a pitch Srinath, till then an unknown cricketer, routed the Maharashtra team with a haul of seven for 93. At the other end, the other tall paceman, also an unknown, was Venkatesh Prasad. He bagged two wickets.

It was the next match that shook Rahul and other youngsters' faith in sportsmanship. The Karnataka team travelled to Kolkata to play Bengal in the quarterfinals. Bengal had a strong and experienced team. Pranob Roy, the current national selector, was the captain. The team also consisted of Arun Lal, Srikanth Kalyani, Ashok Malhotra, Snehasish Ganguly and his brother, the young Saurav, among others.

Karnataka batted first on the Eden Gardens pitch. Skipper Syed Kirmani made a century. Rahul, promoted ahead of Jeshwanth, came in at number six to partner Arjun Raja. The duo batted a whole day without getting out. Rahul struggled a bit initially. But once he found his feet he looked refreshingly hungry and keen to go on. Arjun too was that kind of a batsman. He made 267 and Rahul 134. The pair put on 299 runs before being separated. Jeshwanth made a rapid unbeaten 119 and Karnataka declared at staggering 791 for six.

It was then that Bengal unleashed their gamesmanship and shocked the young Karnataka side. One of the youngsters then said they had come to play a hard game. They expected a tough fight. But some of the things that went on over the next couple of days were simply nauseating and horrified them.

Bengal, those days, was mockingly called a team of quotient champions. It was not always fair, for they certainly had a number of talented cricketers. But at times it looked like they were happier playing the quotient rather than the game out there in the middle. That distant day at the Eden Gardens it was just that. The batsmen kept wasting time and the umpires just did not pull them up. At other times they asked the sight screen to be moved but strangely there was no groundstaff around to do their job. When the Karnataka reserves tried to help out with the movement of the sightscreen they were pelted with banana and orange peels, booed and abused. When the groundsmen surfaced after a lot of time they always did not seem to know in which direction the batsmen wanted the sightscreen moved.

Even with the sightscreen in the accepted place, there often seemed to be somebody or the other who would move across it and bring the game to a standstill.

This apart, the Bengal batsman Snehasish Ganguly hobbled around and called for a runner. He then constantly took so much of time to move from the striker's crease to his position near the square leg umpire that it made mockery of the game. Bengal clung on to make 652 for nine, thanks to Srikant Kalyani's heroic 260 and Snehasish's unbeaten 116, and advanced on quotient. Immediately after the last ball was bowled one of the umpires was chaired by the spectators. The whole last day's play was a travesty of fair play and Karnataka lodged a protest against Bengal's time-wasting tactics. It was of no avail.

Karnataka lost that game, but the match itself served to open the eyes of a number of youngsters in the team. Their romantic notions of sportsmanship were destroyed on that day. Bengal's gamesmanship helped toughen out the Karnataka youngsters in double quick time.

Rahul, meanwhile, had arrived as a first-class player. He had passed the test gloriously in two tough encounters that were fought tooth and nail. Sujith, who at that stage was reckoned to be ahead of Rahul in ability and talent, made 29, 27 and 9 in the three innings in the knock-out while Rahul's two outings fetched him 82 and 134 when batting under pressure. After these innings he simply went from strength to strength.

One of the first to realise that Rahul was something special was Jeshwanth. The left-hand all-rounder was to lead Karnataka for a while. He was a shrewd student of the game and there were many who had time for his opinions.

I remember that distant evening at the Eden Gardens when he told me: "After GR Vishwanath and Brijesh Patel this kid will become the third biggest batting name in Karnataka cricket. He will surpass all the others, Binny, Sudhakar Rao, Jayaprakash, et al." This was high praise for a 17 year-old just breaking into first-class cricket, particularly as he was being talked in the same breath as some of the household names in Indian cricket.

As subsequent events were to prove, Jeshwanath was not wide off the mark. Rahul, in fact, exceeded his predictions. By all accounts Rahul has already surpassed Patel in batsmanship. The pedestal that GR Vishwanath, the artist supreme, occupies is in his sights. Only time can tell whether he would surpass the original little master.

Rahul, by now, was steadily surging ahead. The following year he scored centuries in his first two innings. His first four innings in Ranji Trophy had yielded 82, 134, 126 and 128 runs.

Usually youngsters who break into any team at a higher level struggle to keep their place in the side. They are in and out of the team till they come to terms with that level of the game. In Rahul's case he had already made a mark and did not have to worry about keeping his place in the side. Instead, he was looking forward to bigger things like a berth in the South Zone team for the Duleep Trophy, a place in the Irani Trophy team and a spot as emerging player in teams playing side games against visiting Test teams.

A Lifting Experience

Breaking into the Karnataka team at that stage was to have a huge positive influence on Rahul. It was a team comprising great youngsters, each pushing and goading one another. There was, besides Rahul and Sujith, Kumble, Srinath, Venkatesh Prasad and Arjun Raja. The senior-most player was Kirmani who had this knack of instantly making the youngsters feel comfortable. Jeshwanth, Carlton Saldanha, Raghuram Bhat and Ananth were also easy to get along with.

Then there was Arjun Raja. Affectionately called 'Bozo', he was a terrific character. He kept the spirits of the team high at all times. There was never a dull moment with him around. He cracked jokes all the time and had a most infectious laugh. Though he was a highly successful batsman for Karnataka, he decided somewhere down the line that cricket was not for him. He was a brilliant student and adept in co-curricular activities. He dropped the game one fine day and moved to the Middle East in chase of economic rewards.

Arjun had a big hand in ensuring that a 17-year-old, shy and withdrawn Rahul was made to feel at home in the Karnataka dressing room.

"The train journeys those days were fantastic. It went a long way in bonding and building team spirit. Vishy (GR Vishwanath) who travelled extensively with us as selector and team manager regaled us with fantastic one-liners. He and Kiri related a number of cricket stories and incidents. There was so much of discussion on cricket that we learnt all the time. The amount we picked up in that casual atmosphere was unbelievable.

"The work ethic in the nets too was fantastic. Everybody wanted to get into the Indian team and we were all pushing each other. The best thing was nobody was getting intimidated by the big names, but actually learning a lot from them," said Rahul.

This team spirit and bonding was a great boost for young Rahul. Coming from a loosely organised under-19 setup he was walking into a superb cricket culture with all the players around him highly ambitious.

Another great advantage at this point of his career for the emerging batsman was the presence of some very good fast bowlers in the Karnataka nets. Srinath, Venkatesh Prasad and left-arm pace man Nasiruddin were all tall, young, ambitious and quick. Nasiruddin, till a recurring groin injury laid him low, looked as good as any of the bowlers. An older KG Sekhar revelled in the swing and seam department. Soon, these bowlers were followed by David Johnson, Dodda Ganesh and Mansoor Ali Khan.

With such an impressive array of fast bowlers, Rahul got plenty of practice. He made it really pay for him by encouraging them to bowl whatever they wished to. This was very unlike most other batsmen who asked pacemen to bowl only half-volleys in the nets. Rahul, though, enjoyed taking on the pacemen in the nets and at that young age he really was soaking into some quality practice time.

In any case, with a bowler of Johnson's temperament around, a batsman either had to shape up or ship out. Johnson hated batsmen, whether in the nets or in matches. If any batsman asked him to bowl a half-volley in nets, he was just as likely to get a short-pitched delivery hurled from 20 yards. Johnson, as a pace bowler, was quick. Avinash Vaidya, the Karnataka wicketkeeper, was convinced that he was quicker than Srinath. His deliveries used to skid off the pitch. He used to call his bouncers the throat-ball. He regularly hit a lot of batsmen with short-pitched deliveries. In the Karnataka vs South Africa warm-up game at Kochi he even gave Gary Kirsten a knock on the head.

The thing that went against Johnson, though, was that he was a difficult person to handle. He was explosive, and not just on the cricket field. He had walked out of the MRF Pace Academy in Chennai stating that they had nothing new to teach him. In South Africa, with the Indian team, he had shoulder-charged the Manager, Madan Lal, in the hotel corridor. And although he bagged five wickets in the match against Free State, he was sent back home.

Rahul, apparently was the only batsman who tamed Johnson in the nets. He would goad him and have him come steaming in. It made for fascinating play. Rahul would be all concentration and play only the deliveries he had to. Even if the ball was slightly outside the line of the stumps, he would let it go. He encouraged not just Johnson, but the other pacemen in the nets to bowl whatever they wanted, even from 20 yards. The only demand Rahul made, even at that young age, was that the bowler ought to be serious and try and get him out. He spoke sharply whenever somebody fooled around while bowling to him. In short, he was a man with a mission and he ensured that the others got the message.

In this Rahul benefited when Roger Binny was made coach of the state outfit. Binny, like Daljit Singh before him, emphasised on physical conditioning. Binny would also train with the team and ensure that they got a lot of cross-sport training (Binny had a partiality for football) as a way of relaxation. All the time though the onus was on getting fitter and building up stamina.

On the count of suppleness and agility, Rahul, like the rest of the Karnataka team, and later the Indian team, depended on Yoga expert Dr Omkar, a PhD in the Department of Aerospace at the highly acclaimed Indian Institute of Science (IISc). Rahul studiously worked with Omkar for suppleness, used the KSCA Club House Gymnasium for muscle-toning and strength, and then was at the nets most of the other time. Thus, during those formative years, when he was not playing matches, he was dedicatedly pursuing a course that would hone his cricketing skills.

During this period the rest of the Karnataka team was also coming along nicely. Another crop of younger players, Sunil Joshi, Vijay Bharadwaj, Somashekar Shiruguppi and J Arunkumar, was also blending well with Rahul, Kumble, Srinath, Prasad, Johnson, Ganesh and Sujith, and they were lifting each other's quality of play.

Gradually, Karnataka was once again making waves on the national scene. In 1992-93 they lost by a mere five runs in the knock-out pre-quarter-final to Sandeep Patil-led Madhya Pradesh. The following year they lost on first innings in the quarter-final to Ravi Shastri-led Mumbai.

Meanwhile Rahul, who had a couple of poor seasons in Duleep Trophy, made up for it while playing for the India Under-19 against New Zealand Colts and in the Irani Trophy for Rest of India.

In the 1994-95 season he played just one Ranji Trophy match, against Andhra, and scored 191. Elsewhere, he got his first Irani Trophy century, an unbeaten 132 against Mumbai for Rest of India, and his first Duleep Trophy century, a 148 for South Zone against Central Zone in Jamsedpur.

Rahul, during that year, played a lot of other cricket too. He had broken into the India A team and was the best batsman in the championship—winning for the Saarc Trophy in Dhaka. He also featured prominently in the India A squad that took on England A at home. (See chapter 'Things Fall in Place') Rahul, thus, through his performances forced his way into the Indian World Cup probables squad that trained in Bangalore. Even if he did not make the World Cup squad, it was to be an important inclusion.

Chapter 12

No Half Measures

Rahul had done all the hard work and earned a place among the Indian probables for the 1996 World Cup in the subcontinent. He had succeeded at all levels that he had been thrown into, including against the visiting New Zealand team. Rahul, picked for the Board President's XI, had slammed an unbeaten 145 to highlight his talent and stake a claim for inclusion in the Indian World Cup line-up.

Though he was just 22 years of age at that stage, Rahul was a genuine contender for a batsman's slot in the Indian team. The probables camp was held in Bangalore at the KSCA Stadium. Increasingly it looked like he was doing as well as some of the other, more experienced batsmen in the setup. It was then that a whispering campaign was unleashed against him.

Perhaps the apprehension was that with GR Vishwanath, the Chairman of the National Selection Committee, also hailing from Karnataka, Rahul would be inducted into the side ahead of some other favourites. Whatever the reason, a whole lot of planted stories about his suitability for longer duration matches, rather than limited overs cricket, started appearing in a section of the press. Television discussions too centred on this line of thinking. The surprising aspect was that he was a virtual nobody at that stage, and yet so much of attention was being turned on him.

When the time came to announce the Indian team, Rahul's name did not figure in the team. He had done very well at every stage of the game that year. He had got runs in Ranji Trophy, Duleep Trophy, India A and in the match against New Zealand, and yet was not in the squad.

"I would have loved to be part of the team. At that time I was very disappointed at not being included. But at the start of the season when

I had drawn my goals for the year, I had taken a realistic look at my chances and ruled out being chosen for the World Cup. My goal for that year was to get into the Indian team for the tour of England after the World Cup.

"Having said that, I gave it my best shot at the probables camp. But I knew I would be competing with Sanjay Manjrekar and Vinod Kambli for that berth in the World Cup squad. They had been there at that level of the game and delivered. I was untried. I knew that at such a huge tournament the selectors would not experiment and would instead settle for experience. That's why I had not put down making the World Cup team as one of my goals for the season," said Rahul.

Rahul did not have time to sit and mop about not being picked for the World Cup side. He had missed a few Ranji Trophy league matches because of the probables camp and now that he was not in the Indian team, he was free to return to the Karnataka side. He played the last South Zone league match against Tamil Nadu before the knock-out phase of the tournament started.

The KSCA Stadium, where the Indian probables had their camp, was being modified for the World Cup. The pavilion, dressing rooms, stands were being done up, light towers were being put up for the day-night encounter, the stands were being given a coat of paint and the pitch and square were being tended to. With the KSCA Stadium thus not available for the Ranji Trophy tournament, the knock-out matches were staged at the nearby RSI grounds.

Although the RSI grounds belonged to the military, there was little security on display there. Thus, when Karnataka played Baroda, there was little or no privacy for the players. The spectators had easy access to the players, and this was not always a good thing.

One afternoon during the lunch break when Rahul and his childhood friend Fazal Khaleel, who had made his Ranji Trophy debut earlier that year, were relaxing, a couple of spectators approached them, stood over Rahul and started abusing him.

"We were sitting when they came and first started talking about his batting. They had read the campaign against him by a section of the media during the World Cup selection phase, and their mob mentality had taken over," said Fazal. "I looked at Rahul even as these two guys passed comments, abuse and ridicule but he did not utter a single word. He just continued looking at them with a deadpan expression. I was seething. I could not tolerate it further. I stood up to hit them, not bothered about the consequences. But Rahul pulled me down and said 'just sit tight. I'll speak to you later.' After a lot more abusing, and seeing that they were getting no response from him, they just walked away. KSCA organised security only much later.

"After they left, Rahul said: 'Relax. I wanted to know what the public felt about me. Now I got part of the opinion first hand. You know, some of the things those guys said are true. It is not all abuse. I think I need to improve in a few areas.'

"Even though I have known Rahul since childhood the cold logic with which he addressed the issue floored me. It confirmed my belief further that he was unlike anybody I knew," said Fazal.

Rahul, in that match and the earlier one against Bengal, had not scored too many runs. But by the time the semi-finals came he was in smashing form. Leading the team also gave him plenty to do. Three Karnataka players, Anil Kumble, Javagal Srinath and Venkatesh Prasad, were doing World Cup duty with the Indian team. Raghuram Bhat had retired. But along came the nippy David Johnson, Dodda Ganesh and a young left-arm spinner who could bat in the person of Sunil Joshi. They, along with off spinner R Ananth, ensured that Rahul did not feel the absence of the three top bowlers. The RSI pitch which had bounce and pace also helped the Karnataka attack better.

Rahul made a splendid 153 in the semi-finals against Hyderabad, a match that Karnataka easily won on first innings. Rahul had led the team to the final and had enjoyed the task. But for the final, against Tamil Nadu, the three stars were back in the team after their World Cup campaign had ended, and Kumble was once again given the honour of leading Karnataka.

"Leading Karnataka to the final and later starring in my first Ranji Trophy triumph took away some of the pain and disappointment of not making the World Cup squad," confessed Rahul. He had made another century in the final and thereby reminded the national selectors that he was around and in cracking touch.

They finally took note of his prowess and rewarded him with a place in the Indian team (see chapter 'The Great Wall of Indian Cricket').

Rahul did not play Ranji Trophy cricket the following season as he was in the thick of international cricket. However, in 1997-98, between the home series against Sri Lanka and Australia (when Sachin Tendulkar devastated Shane Warne), he once again led Karnataka.

It was the period when Indian selections defied logic. Javagal Srinath who had injured his shoulder in the West Indies was replaced by a Hyderabad cricketer called Noel David. How a player of his average ability and talent earned a national call would remain one of the mysteries of Indian cricket. Likewise, the selection of Sairaj Bahutule, Hrishikesh Kanitkar, Rahul Sanghvi and some of the others under one pretext or the other raised a lot of eyebrows. In this scenario, Rahul was dropped for the one-dayers against Sri Lanka and later Australia. This axing came despite Rahul having had a very good Test series against them. Subsequently, he was omitted from the Indian team that took part in the limited overs tournament in Sharjah. The excuse the selectors gave was that his game was more suited to Tests. It naturally led to a lot of protests.

Whatever, Rahul now became available to again lead Karnataka's quest for Ranji Trophy success. He smashed a superb 215 in the final against Uttar Pradesh to stamp his class all over again. He led the team with much passion that season. He set goals and drove the team to meeting them.

The toughest game for Karnataka and Rahul that season came in the semi-finals against Hyderabad on a substandard Secunderabad pitch. Both teams had their main players—Hyderabad's Mohammed Azharuddin and VVS Laxman, and Karnataka's Kumble, Srinath and Prasad—turning out for India in the one-day tri-series against Australia and Zimbabwe. All Karnataka players felt that their Skipper Rahul too ought to have been with the national team rather than at the Secunderabad grounds. With then National Selector Shivlal Yadav watching the game, they were itching to put it across Hyderabad. But the match took its own turn.

For starters, Hyderabad won the toss and chose to bat. That itself guaranteed that they were to be in the driving seat in the match. Their top order, which had a number of fine batsmen in Skipper MV Sridhar, Vanka Pratap, Daniel Manohar, Nand Kishore and Arvind Shetty, did the side a great service by posting 283. It was not a great total. But on that track it was something the two Hyderabad spinners, former Test player Venkatpathy Raju and Kanwaljit Singh, appreciated.

Karnataka too began well with a century opening partnership between Sujith Somasundar and an aggressive J Arunkumar. But once they were gone, it was Hyderabad that had the upper hand.

"We lost a few quick wickets before Rahul joined me out in the middle," said Fazal Khaleel, the number three batsman for Karnataka. "We had a good partnership going. Rahul was batting superbly, but I took my chances. I knew the pitch was deteriorating and if we got bogged down Kanwaljit and Venkatpathy would get right on top. There was about 30 minutes to go for the close of play that day and Rahul must have come down the pitch and spoken to me at least 15 times to take it easy and not throw away my wicket. Then in the last over of the day I swept Kanwaljit to the fence. Rahul once again came down the track and told me to stop playing like this. 'There are just five balls to go. Just hang on or give me the strike,' he said. Next ball, I again tried to sweep, bottom-edged onto my pad and was caught at silly point.

"Rahul went ballistic. He abused me from the wicket to the pavilion, in the dressing room, in the bus, en route to the hotel and in the hotel. I was stunned. Yes, I'd got out. But this was just a game. But he would have nothing of it. He kept shouting that if I did not know how to defend it was better for me to give up the game and do something else in life.

"That hurt. It really hurt. He was not ticking me off in private, but in front of the players, the opponents, the umpires, the media, spectators, my friends, everybody. I mean this was my best friend, somebody whom I grew up with from childhood. I had never seen him like this. I swore I'd never talk to him again in my life," recalled Fazal.

Karnataka squeezed out a small lead with skipper Rahul leading from the front with an invaluable knock of 71. They dismissed Hyderabad a second time and had a relatively low score of 154 to get for a win.

On the fourth evening Karnataka were 48 for two when Rahul came out to join Fazal at the wicket. By now everybody knew the captain and his best friend were not on talking terms. Fazal was out to prove to his skipper that he had a defence and Rahul remained his usual defensive self. They went about their job without saying a word to each other.

"At the end of the day's play I told him that I would speak to him only after we won the match," Fazal recalled.

Rahul was dismissed early the next morning while Fazal departed after making 51. Karnataka suddenly slipped to 127 for eight.

"We were never in the game after we had lost the toss. Except for Rahul, Ganesh and Mansoor, everybody realised that. It was very tense in the dressing room at lunch on the last day. We had just one wicket in hand and still needed a few runs.

"The crowd was against us. The tension was unbearable. Nobody in our team ate or drank anything at lunch. Everybody was piling on pressure on Ganesh and Mansoor. But Rahul conducted himself superbly. He spoke calmly. He calmed down things in the dressing room, but kept the last pair focused and with their adrenalin pumping. He knew they'd need it out there. We finally managed to pull off the win by the skin of the teeth. It was as much a tribute to Ganesh and Mansoor's never-say-die spirit as it was to Rahul's leadership," said Fazal.

After that nail-biting win, Rahul and Karnataka were unstoppable and lifted the Ranji Trophy for the second time in three years.

"Winning the Ranji Trophy has certainly been one of the high points of my career. Every single first class cricketer would like to be a part of the national championship-winning team. I had already been part of the winning team in 1996. Yet, when I led this fine bunch of talented cricketers of Karnataka to success in 1998 it was extremely satisfying," said Rahul.

Chapter 13

The Great Wall of Indian Cricket

Young Rahul was overlooked for the 1996 World Cup only because the selectors preferred experience to youth. However, after India lost in the semi-finals to Sri Lanka (Lanka were awarded the match after the Eden Gardens crowd turned violent and halted play) the selectors decided that they had to bring in some fresh blood. The best of the emerging lot, as far as batsmen were concerned, was Rahul and they picked him for the back-to-back one-day tours to Singapore and Sharjah.

India, Pakistan and Sri Lanka competed for the Singer Trophy in Singapore and India, Pakistan and South Africa battled it out for the Pepsi Cup in Sharjah. It was not a very happy sojourn for Rahul as his highest score in four innings was 11. And he was sent in at number eight in that match against South Africa.

The good thing about those tours, though, was that it helped Rahul to break into the pack. He had undergone a strenuous World Cup probables camp and had bonded well with the other players. His outstanding success in domestic cricket and at the India A level ensured that he did not feel he was gatecrashing into a higher setup.

"At no time did I feel that I did not belong during the tour. I just looked at it as the next natural progression in my career. I had played with and against most of the players in the team, either in domestic cricket or as part of the India A team setup," said Rahul.

Besides, there were three others from his state, Anil Kumble, Javagal Srinath and Venkatesh Prasad, already in the Indian team and they went out of the way to make him feel at home.

Rahul, who batted at number four in his debut match, against Sri Lanka, was snared behind the stumps by that wily fox Muthiah Muralitharan for a paltry three runs.

Though Rahul had broken into the Indian team in the one-dayers, he had really set his sight on the tour to England. That tour was to follow within a few days of the Sharjah tournament and the fact that Rahul was dropped for the matches during the later stages of the tournament did not augur well. This apart, a section of the media was once again sniping at him and another emerging player, Saurav Ganguly.

But the senior selection committee comprising GR Vishwanath (chairman), Anshuman Gaekwad, Sambaran Banerjee, Ravinder Chadha and KM Rungta went ahead and chose both Rahul and Saurav. The selection of Saurav, in particular, attracted a lot of criticism. Much was written against Rahul too being in the team. But Vishwanath was unfazed.

"I knew Rahul was good. I had seen him bat from a pretty young age and I was aware of his potential. But I did not want to impress my views on the other selectors. I was particular that we were selecting the Indian team and others had to judge for themselves the potential of this young boy from my state. I told them to watch him play and assess him first hand. So over a period of time they followed him in Duleep Trophy games, in Ranji Trophy, against visiting sides and in India A matches. One by one they were convinced that he looked good and could be given an opportunity to play in the seniors team.

"The only apprehension was of exposing him to international cricket on a tough tour to England. Would it not be better to blood him in a home series?—was the question that was posed. Should we wait or was it possible that by pushing him we would actually retard his development? These were the posers before us.

"At that time we assessed him. He had come good at every stage of the game. He just grabbed the opportunities that came his way and excelled. The only criticism, if you call it that, was that he took a long time to settle in during every innings.

"We decided that this was an advantage in England as he would get a hang of the pitch conditions. Also, since he had been on two private tours to England (the Kingfisher sponsored tour and with ex-

Test cricketer Kailash Ghattani's Star Cricket Club), Rahul was familiar with the conditions there. Taking all these into consideration, we backed him for that Test tour," reasoned GR Vishwanath.

It turned out to be one of the most inspired pieces of selections made by Vishwanath's committee. By the time that tour came to an end, Rahul was being hailed as one of the finest young batsmen in the game.

For many reasons it was the ideal debut tour for Rahul. There were 18 matches in all, including the three Tests and three One-dayers. On tours when there are very few side games, the seniors want to play all the games to get into some sort of form and stay in touch for the bigger games. This restricts the opportunities for youngsters. But when there are a huge number of side games the youngsters in the team get a good look-in. They also get a chance to force their way back into the Test side, in case they get bumped off after a Test or two.

Rahul, in fact, played 11 matches for 591 runs and had the third highest tour average of 53.72. Only Saurav and Tendulkar had a better average. Rahul also played two One-dayers against Holland on that tour.

That year England enjoyed a glorious summer, with very few match days spoilt by rain. The only sour point was that he was pushed into wicketkeeping. He had not kept for seven years by then, if the couple of Duleep Trophy matches where he chipped in as emergency wicketkeeper before the tour were discounted. Nayan Mongia was the main wicketkeeper on the tour, with batsman Sanjay Manjrekar supposed to be his stand-in. Mongia, though, injured his hand and Manjrekar lost interest in keeping. Rahul, therefore, had to stand in a couple of side games, and he did it with gloves borrowed from Mongia.

"I was a ball-stopper, really. I was not mentally prepared for the task and saw it only as a one-off thing. But at that stage of your career you are willing to do anything to get into the national team that I kept wickets most enthusiastically," said Rahul. Little did he know then that wicketkeeping was soon going to play a major role in his cricketing career.

The tour started quietly enough for Rahul. He played in the second tour match against England's National Cricket Academy and made an unbeaten 16. Against Gloucestershire he made an unbeaten 86 and

28. He did not play the first two one-dayers, which India lost. He and Saurav were instead included for the third at the expense of Manjrekar and Navjot Sidhu, both of whom were a liability when it came to running between the wickets.

Rahul made an unbeaten 22 in that third one-dayer, which India lost again. But the stir caused at that game was by Sidhu who walked out of the tour after being dropped. Apparently he was not informed that he was not playing and had padded up to go and bat when the sniggers by some insensitive members of the Indian team got to him. He felt humiliated and walked out of the team.

Rahul did not get to play the first Test, but in the preceding match he had scored an unbeaten 58 and had shared in a 153-run unbroken stand with Skipper Mohammed Azharuddin (111 n.o.).

India lost the first Test and were a demoralised side. They had lost all the one-dayers, lost the first Test, seen an experienced Sidhu walk out and their wicketkeeper too was laid low. Sunil Joshi had injured his hand and was being sent back to India. To compound it, Manjrekar had injured an ankle and did not look fit when the second Test loomed large. It was a gloomy situation for the Indian team. It was in such a scenario that the team met.

"On the eve of the match, at the team meeting it was decided that Saurav would make his debut. Azhar told me that I would play the Test in case Sanjay failed the fitness Test," revealed Rahul.

On the morning of the match Manjrekar was found unfit and Rahul got his chance to make his Test debut at Lord's.

"I was mentally geared to play the night before the Test. So when the call came I was not too surprised. On the morning of the match, I remember walking down the stairs of Lord's and telling myself, I am Indian Test player number 207. Whatever happens from here nobody can take that away from me. Luckily we fielded first. I got my chance to bat two days later. By that time I had become a bit more ambitious," Rahul said recalling the biggest moment of his cricket career.

England took strike and made 344. When India replied, Saurav, the other debutant, batted beautifully at number three. Watching him bat gave Rahul a lot of confidence. He knew that he too could handle the stuff at this level of the game. Saurav made an impressive century on debut. Rahul, who came in at number seven, got into a 94-run stand with him. They batted brilliantly and lifted the spirits of the team. Suddenly there was a lot of youthful vigour in the batting.

Rahul was nervous to start with. But after the first fifteen minutes he batted like a dream. Saurav made 131 while Rahul missed his debut century by a mere five runs. "I was kicking myself for having got out at 95. Later someone told me that if I had made those five runs it would have been a world record: two debutants getting a century in the same match on debut," said Rahul.

Rahul and Saurav's coming good was very vital to the side's moral. They were already without Sidhu. The makeshift opener Nayan Mongia was not having a good time. Ajay Jadeja and Vikram Rathore looked unsuitable for the job as openers. There was tremendous pressure on the rest of the batsmen. At a time like this, the outstanding success enjoyed by Saurav and Rahul came as a blessing,

Saurav made another century in the third Test. Sachin Tendulkar blasted 177. Rahul, who once again came late in the order, tried to get the tail-end batsmen to hang in there with him. He had a good partnership with Venkatesh Prasad (13) and, with last man Venkatpathy Raju, was inching towards his maiden Test century when he nicked one to the keeper. Rahul made 84 and had arrived as a batsman. India lost the Test series 1-0. Rahul and Saurav, both young and looking very classy, were the finds of the tour for India.

"I met Rahul as soon as he returned home," said Fazal Khaleel his childhood friend. "We had met likewise after he had made his Ranji Trophy debut. At that time he'd said 'I'm now a first-class cricketer'. This time around, I told him he was a Test cricketer, and queried, what next? It was then that Rahul spoke of his ambition: 'I do not want to be just another Test cricketer. I have made the grade, yes. So have dozens of others. When I retire I want to be bracketed with Sunil Gavaskar and GR Vishwanath'."

It is this kind of clear focus that has made Rahul a cricketer with a difference. He sets goals for himself very early, is not shy of speaking about it, and then goes about doing everything necessary; including all the hard work and sacrifice, to ensure that he gives himself a chance to achieve his goals.

Of course, many who speak of their goals and aims could often be labelled as boastful or vain and all-talk. But this would not apply to

Rahul. For one, he opens out only to those he knows well and is comfortable with. With him speaking of his goals is a quiet but firm expression of his burning desire. And watching him prepare for the task is a revelation in itself.

Despite this, Rahul's next couple of series, a one-off Test against Australia in New Delhi and three Tests against South Africa at home, were quite damp. He came up with a knock of 56 on a poor Kanpur pitch, his only half century in seven innings. The Indian team management tried to experiment and unexpectedly asked him to open the batting against South Africa at Kolkata. Rahul made 31 and 23, but was not comfortable in the role.

There was hardly any time before the team embarked on their tour to South Africa and Rahul tried to make the best use of this short time by trying to practise in conditions that afforded the sort of bounce and pace he would have to tackle there. He got a few players to bounce a wet tennis ball off the slate-covered flooring at the KSCA Stadium pavilion. Batting in this manner prepared him better than a long stint at the slow, low-bounce Kanpur could have.

"We don't have anybody who bowls at that pace. Besides our pitches too do not have the same bounce and pace that could be expected in South Africa. The wet tennis ball practice on the pavilion steps of KSCA was one of the ways to simulate their conditions," opined Rahul.

The South Africans who had been humiliated in the series in India were thirsting for revenge. The Indian team coming over so soon was ideal for the purpose. The South Africans scheduled the side games on flat pitches and threw in only lesser bowlers against the Indian batsmen. Yet when it came to the Tests they ensured that the pitches provided plenty of pace and bounce to their superb quartet of Allan Donald, Shaun Pollock, Lance Klusner and Brian McMillan.

Rahul looked pretty comfortable against the Proteas pacemen, though the quantum of runs did not reflect that. He had opened without success in the second Test. Skipper Tendulkar asked him to bat at number three for the final Test at the Wanderers Stadium in Johannesburg. By now, although Rahul had played just eight Tests, he had been shunted to bat at all spots, from opening to number seven.

He had also not scored a Test century till then, and saw this number three slot as an opportunity to take his time to settle down and score at his pace. At number three there was no fear of the brittle tail leaving him high and dry, or his having to farm the bowling.

India had already lost the series 2-0 and were playing only for their pride. They opened the batting with Vikram Rathore and Nayan Mongia. Rahul came in to bat soon enough and was given a torrid welcome on a juicy pitch by Donald, Pollock, Klusner and McMillan.

"I had made up my mind. If I got stuck in there for a while I was not going to come back without a big score. I suddenly started enjoying playing these pacemen. It was a challenge, but I was enjoying myself immensely," said Rahul.

His technique and powers of concentration were tested to the full. However, he was in no hurry to score the runs. He batted a long, long time and after six hours reached his century. It was his first in Tests, and coming on a tough tour against a world-class bowling and fielding side in conditions hostile to batsmen it gave him immense confidence in his ability.

"I remember it was a greatly satisfying hundred. I had faced up to the challenge and come good. Besides as an emerging cricketer you look forward to playing your first Test. After that you look forward to your first Test hundred. With that century in Johannesburg I had put those two desires behind me and could now set my sights on bigger things," recalled Rahul.

He followed his knock of 148 with a quick-fire 81 in the second innings. The Indians were setting a target and wanted quick runs on the board. Rahul shifted to a higher gear and played some lovely cricket. However, the much-awaited win did not come through as Darryl Cullinan and the rains ensured that the South Africans clung on to a draw.

For Rahul it was a satisfying series. It was his second official tour overseas and, like in England earlier, he had passed the test with flying colours.

A couple of weeks later he was in the Indian team for an equally challenging series—against West Indies in West Indies. Now the Caribbean calypsos might have slipped a notch or two from their lofty pedestal of the 80s, but they still had pacemen of the skill of Curtly

Ambrose, Courtney Walsh and Ian Bishop. The batting revolved around Brian Lara, with Carl Hooper, Shivnaraine Chanderpaul and Stuart Williams propping up the side time and again.

A couple of years earlier, Walsh and company with their brand of aggressive fast bowling had virtually finished Vinod Kambli's international career in the series in India, and could be expected to try and dent a few other reputations too.

Under the circumstances, Rahul gave a fine account of himself in that series. Coming in at his new-found number three spot he got amongst the runs in almost all the innings. He came close to scoring a century on a couple of occasions. But it was not be. The first couple of Tests at Kingston, Jamaica, and Port of Spain, Trinidad, petered out into draws. The moment of reckoning for the Indian team came at Bridgetown, Barbados.

The pitch was two-bounce, two-pace. It deteriorated as the game progressed. The West Indies batted first and only Chanderpaul's 137 saved them from disaster. They made a healthy 298 to put pressure on India.

When India batted, Skipper Tendulkar (92) and Rahul (78) added 170 runs for the third wicket. Both batted gloriously against the pace of Ambrose, Bishop, Mervyn Dillon and Franklyn Rose. But once they were dismissed, the rest of the batsmen, Ganguly, Azharuddin, Mongia, all blew it. Only Kumble (23 n.o.) put up some sort of fight. India made 319, a lead of 21. But considering the fact that they would have to bat last on a rapidly deteriorating pitch, the Indians had as good as messed it up. Still, the Indian bowlers, Venkatesh Prasad, Abhey Kuruvilla and Dodda Ganesh, tried to make a fight of it. Lara slammed a chancy 45 but the home team was still tottering at 107 for nine, just 86 runs ahead. It was then that the last wicket pair of Ambrose (18 n.o.) and Dillon (21) threw their bats around to add an invaluable 33 runs.

Set to make a paltry 120 for a win, the Indians were never in the fight. They were mesmerised by the two-bounce pitch. Rahul was caught behind by a delivery that flew off a length. That so psyched some of the others that they started addressing the bounce rather than playing the ball on its merit. Only VVS Laxman (19) got into double figures. India were bundled out for 81. With the next two Tests in

Antigua and Georgetown, Guyana, hampered by rain, the Indians had lost their best chance to win. It was a defeat that rankles Rahul to this day.

"It was not an impossible pitch to bat on. We could so easily have got more runs in the first innings. Even in the second I think we played well below par," he said.

In the subsequent Tests against Sri Lanka and Australia in the subcontinent, Rahul, even if he did not score a century, was getting plenty of big scores: 69, 92, 93, 85, 52, 56 and 86. He went through 13 Tests before registering his second hundred, a 118 against Zimbabwe at Harare. Later that season, he blasted a century in each innings—190 and 103—against New Zealand at Hamilton. By then he was already reckoned to be the Great Wall of Indian cricket.

His impeccable defence, sound technique and temperament and willingness to occupy the crease for a great length of time had marked him out as the fulcrum around which the Indian batting revolved. Yes, the Indian batting line-up boasted of Tendulkar, Azharuddin, Ganguly, Sidhu and Laxman. But Rahul's value to the team increased in proportion to the distance it travelled away from Indian pitches.

Chapter 14

Matchless Record

Most Indian batsmen have floundered overseas. Former greats Sunil Gavaskar and GR Vishwanath towered over the rest of the batsmen of their era mainly because they did well both on Indian pitches and on pitches abroad. The team and its followers soon realised that the team's success was directly proportional to the success of its batsman.

Whenever the Indian batsmen ran up a huge total, they helped the team's bowlers to maintain pressure on the rivals. Of course, when these big totals were posted on the low-bounce, turning tracks of India, it was the Indian spinners who reaped the benefit. The spinners, even the medium pacers, could have been effective on foreign pitches too, except that the Indian batsmen seldom gave their own bowlers the luxury of defending big totals.

For instance, Anil Kumble's overseas record as a bowler is freely criticised by the media without appreciating that he has taken more than a hundred Test wickets in matches abroad. The fact that few other Indian bowlers have aggregated hundred Test wickets both at home and overseas put together is conveniently ignored. For that matter, few speak of the corresponding overseas record of the batsmen of Kumble's era. Barring Rahul and Sachin Tendulkar, the others, Mohammed Azharrudin, Navjot Sidhu, Saurav Ganguly, Sanjay Manjrekar, Vinod Kambli, et al., have been more comfortable on subcontinent pitches than the ones elsewhere. Even if they have done well elsewhere, it is just in the odd series.

Rahul, on the other hand, actually has a better record abroad. What makes this record all the more peculiar is that it was only after 29 Tests and five centuries overseas that he succeeded in registering his first Test hundred at home.

One reason was that he seldom got to bat at a fixed position at home. On foreign soil, he mostly batted at the challenging number three position. But in India, where batting conditions were easier, other batsmen grabbed the spot and he was moved up and down the batting line-up like a yo-yo. He opened the batting, came number three or four or five or six, or even seven. While this constant change in batting order might have put off a lesser person, Rahul took it pretty philosophically. He believed that a top batsman should be able to bat at any position and adapt to the needs of the situation, team and position. His belief was that through the strength of his performance he ought to be able to command a spot higher and higher in the batting order.

Having said that, Rahul simply could not understand his discomfort with the task of opening the batting.

"I had never opened the batting at any level—school, college, club or state level—never ever. The first time I opened was when I was asked to in the Kolkata Test against South Africa and subsequently in South Africa. My success rate as an opener has been poor. A lot of people have asked me why, when I have batted at number three and gone in at zero for one and come good, I could not pull it off as an opener. I have no explanation.

"It is just that I'm not comfortable. May be it has something to do with preparing myself for batting. I am so used to preparing myself to batting in a position. Sometimes I feel I do not know how to prepare myself to bat as an opener. May be I try too hard. May be I get too tense and tighten up. I don't know. I only know that in a lot of ways opening the batting is different and a task for a specialist," explained Rahul.

Captains and selectors have seen Rahul succeed gloriously at number three against the new, hard ball and believed that he could pull it off in that opening slot too.

Rahul has handled the bouncing ball better that most as he was brought up on the matting wickets of Bangalore where the bounce was higher. Till the age of 19 most of the cricket he played was on these wickets. Of course, on matting wickets the ball does not skid or seam as it would on a hard or soft turf pitch. The important thing though was that his footwork, balance and technique had adapted to the ball bouncing higher. Besides, there were a number of good fast bowlers in his state, in Javagal Srinath, Venkatesh Prasad, David Johnson, Dodda Ganesh, Nasiruddin and Mansoor Ali Khan, and he gained valuable practice playing these quality bowlers in the nets.

This apart, Rahul's preparations for a major match was amazingly methodical. You'd be forgiven if you thought most of it was elementary. Few batsmen appreciate the importance of preparation for a big match. Rahul, on the other hand, is intense and shows a thoroughness and commitment in preparation that is unmatched in Indian cricket. It used to be said of the late Vijay Merchant that before the official tour to England he used to get up daily at an unearthly hour in Mumbai, and when it was still not yet dawn, would water the pitch and get medium pacers to bowl to him in the dull light. He believed that he was duplicating English conditions and getting used to batting in them. His subsequent success on that tour was attributed to this thorough preparation. Rahul paid even more attention to the detail of preparation.

Rahul would assess the opponents' bowlers, their weakness and strengths. He would then come face to face with his own strengths and weaknesses. His philosophy was that there was nothing wrong with acknowledging your weakness. You could make it work for you if you could learn to face up to it and neutralise it. He believed that the coach was around for just this sort of help in ironing it out and sought to practise accordingly.

He belief was that the selectors picked him because they saw something positive in him. He, therefore, had a duty to prepare himself in terms of fitness, skills and concentration. Getting psychologically conditioned went with the territory for Rahul.

Rahul approached nets with the same seriousness and commitment as walking into a match. He would tell the bowlers, particularly the fast bowlers, to imagine it was a match situation when bowling to him. He would tell them to bowl bouncers without informing him. His line of thinking was that if he went into nets with pads, thigh pads, helmet and all other protective paraphernalia, he should be able to take on any kind of bowling. If he wanted the fast bowlers to bowl just half volleys in the nets then he might as well go and bat with just a 'T' shirt and shorts! He drove this philosophy into his fast bowlers and made them come at him with everything they had.

Rahul's contention was that batting was a process of self-exploration and self-discovery. "You need to realise what the opponents perceive as your weakness. Only then can you plan for the line of attack that is going to come at you. You should prepare for it mentally and in the nets.

"I always believed in talking to former players, coaches and others to get an idea on what I could expect on a particular pitch or tour. I would find out details about the opponents' key bowlers—their strengths, weaknesses, application, commitment, line of thinking, etc. I would then prepare accordingly."

Before every match he would do a little bit of mental exercise, replaying his best innings, his successes against the particular bowler or team or on that pitch. He believed that winning in the mind was a crucial make-up to do battle.

Speaking of the extra bounce and seam movement and the manner in which he overcame it, Rahul believed that repetitive exposure to these could do the trick.

"In India we see so little of the seaming ball and the extra bounce that we seem at a loss when we first come across it. You need to see more and more of it until tackling it properly becomes second nature, where your instincts take over. It is actually the same as playing spin bowling. We see so much of it that we are not fazed when we see the ball popping and turning. Likewise, we have to ensure that our balance, technique and shot selection are spot on when playing the bouncing ball," observed Rahul.

Of course, having seen so little of the ball bouncing constantly over waist-high, Indian batsmen are at a loss when it comes to letting the ball go. They are not sure which deliveries to play and which to let pass to the wicketkeeper. Besides, on slow Indian wickets batsmen get away with playing across the line or away from the body. But on quick or seaming tracks the batsmen end up paying for these indiscretions, even if at times they seem minor.

Rahul,. therefore, pays great attention to these details. He knows that he must get the basics right again and again, or at the highest level he would be prised out. The wet-tennis ball manoeuvre or getting the fast bowlers to deliver from 20 yards is part of his strategy to ensure that he does not stray from the basics in crunch situations.

At one time he also tried altering the balance of the bat. Of course, he later dismissed it as nothing, but it is a reflection of the detail he goes into in preparation for a tour. Apparently, once during the Australians' tour of India, he picked up Ricky Ponting's bat during the drinks break and found that it had a different feel. He instantly surmised that the meat or sweat spot on that bat was higher, unlike his bat which, to accommodate the lower bounce of Indian tracks, was lower down the bat.

Rahul then felt that the balance of the Australians' bat was wrong to succeed on Indian pitches, just as he believed that he ought to get a different set of bats to come good in Australia. The plan was to shift the sweat spot higher so that it could accommodate the higher bounce on the Australia pitches. He flew down to Jallandar and worked with his bat manufacturer to alter the bat balance for his trip to Australia. "But I did not use it," he said. "I did not like the feel. I tried it in the nets, but was not comfortable with the balance. May be I was not used to it."

Rahul uses an amazingly light bat. Certainly this comes in very handy to play the hook and square cut against the fast bowlers. The lightness of the bat also stands him in good stead over his extended vigils at the crease. A heavy bat would only feel heavier as the innings progressed and make the arm, wrist and fingers weary over a length of time. Rahul also believes that with a heavier bat a batsman would not pay sufficient heed to the basics. Sooner or later those with a heavier bat would fall into a tendency of driving without stretching or leading with the front shoulder. This could open a whole range of other defects.

For all the preparation, though, Rahul did not enjoy a successful tour of Australia in 1999-2000. He had met with success all over the world, but lost the plan a bit in Australia and ended with just 93 runs from three Tests.

"To be fair I was not playing well at that time. And against Australia there was no escape route. They make you pay for your sloppiness. Unlike other teams when you can hope for an over or two of respite, against the Australians there are no easy overs, no easy runs. They come at you all the time. Their bowlers are all outstanding and the fielding very sharp. So if you are not at your peak all the time, you are sunk. I feel that against a team like that you also need a bit of luck to come good, especially at the start," reasoned Rahul about his lack of success on that tour.

But Rahul made up for the lack of success against the Aussies in Australia when they toured India the following year. He slammed that superb 180 which beautifully complemented VVS Laxman's knock of 281. The record-breaking 376-run stand between them thwarted the all-conquering Aussies and helped end their 16-Test winning streak.

Rahul's ability to stay focused is a great asset, especially when he is at the batting crease. He is seldom troubled by sledging, and actually believes that a lit bit of 'chat' is good for the game. It should be stopped only if it looks like degenerating into something else he believes.

"We are the custodians of the game. There are so many children watching matches and following it on television and keeping an eye on their heroes' career that we would let them down if we brought disrepute to the game. A little bit of 'friendly chat' and leg-pulling here and there is okay I feel," he stressed.

▲ *A very young Rahul trying his hand with a full-size bat while practising in a vacant site near his house in Indiranagar.*

► *A freeze of Rahul Dravid taken a few days after his breaking into the Indian team*

▲ *Memories of another day. A very young Rahul (sitting fourth from left), member of the St. Aloysius House (Red) at St. Anthony's Boys School. To his right is childhood friend and classmate Fazal Khaleel.*

▼ Look mom, I made it: *Rahul, seated second from right, after he broke into the school seniors team at the age of 13. To his right is Fazal Khaleel.*

▲ *The Karnataka Under-15 team, winners of the South Zone V Pattabhiraman Trophy in 1988. Rahul is standing sixth from left. To his left are Mahendra, manager and former state player; Keki Tarapore, coach who had a big hand in the development of Rahul and Fazal Khaleel who led the team that year. Three others in that team, A Vijay (kneeling extreme left), K Sriram (third from left) and J Arunkumar (3rd from right and current Karnataka captain) made the first class grade.*

▼ *Cottonian Shield Champions 1987: Rahul (standing extreme right) impeccably dressed as usual with the rest of the St Joseph's Boys School team. Standing in the centre is Father Dennis Coelho the Principal. To his left is former state player and coach Najam Hussain. Kneeling in the centre between the shields is former Indian hockey Olympian Sandeep Somesh. Two places to his right is Fazal Khaleel.*

▲ *A proud moment for the Dravid family: The brothers, Rahul and Vijay, captains of the seniors and juniors St Joseph's Boys School display the Cottonian Shields won by their teams.*

▲ *A rare photo of schoolboy Rahul with his childhood hero, Sunil Gavaskar. Vijay is to Gavaskar's right.*

▲ *The young Rahul's other childhood hero was GR Vishwanath. He and Vijay pose with the legend in this rare informal photo.*

▶ *Fr Dennis Coelho, Rahul's principal at school, pinning the House (Patricks) leader medal on Rahul at the investiture ceremony at St Joseph's Boys School.*

▼ *Rahul is flanked by his coaches, Keki Tarapore (to his right) and former Indian Test batsman Hanumanth Singh.*

▲ *Padded and waiting his turn to bat*

▲ *A classical textbook style of the ball—Rahul Dravid's hallmark Note how he stretches forward totally, covers the flight of ball with his front foot, left shoulder leading towards the pitch of the ball, eye-watching the ball closely with the bat held high out of harm's way.*

◀ *Take that—A leg glance played with feline grace eases past the wicketkeeper*

◀ *A rare photograph of Rahul Dravid showing his moves at the Karnataka State Hockey Association astro-turf Rahul was a keen hockey player till the demands of cricket forced him to give up the game.*

▼ *Rahul and many of the Indian team players take yoga very seriously. Dr. Omkar, yoga exponent (lying on the floor) takes the players through a routine as Rahul, Venkatesh Prasad, Mohammed Kaif, Javagal Srinath, John Wright and Vijay Bhardwaj observe keenly.*

▼ *'Look, he has come dressed 48 hours in advance for the Test,' Rahul Dravid seems to be telling of Sunil Joshi as they and Anil Kumble walk into the stadium.*

▲ *The Karnataka Chief Minister SM Krishna honours Rahul Dravid with the Rajyotsava Award, the highest Karnataka state award, in 2002.*

▲ *Rahul has always supported charitable causes. Freeze of him as Chief Guest at one of Rotary Club of Bangalore's charitable activity*

▲ *Is it just? — asks the legend above a Rahul Dravid poster as his fans protest his dropping on flimsy grounds for a one-day tournament in 1998.*

▼ *Rahul Dravid, India captain for the TVS Cup one-day matches against New Zealand and Australia in the absence of a recuperating Saurav Ganguly, shares a light moment with the Chairman of the National Selection Committee, Syed Kirmani. Rahul made his first class debut for Karnataka under Kirmani.*

▼ *The Dravid family pose at the Wedding reception of Rahul and Vijeeta. Standing are Vijay and his wife Bhavana with Vijeeta and Rahul. Seated are Rahul and Vijay's parents Pushpa and Sharad.*

▲ *An autographed wedding photo of Vijeeta and Rahul.*

▲ *Rahul and Vijeeta in Scotland during their honeymoon in May 2003.*

▲ *Endorsing a sponsor's product*
Rahul has been a model celebrity and a role model for children.

Chapter 15

Leading an Honour

Someone once jokingly remarked that being India's cricket captain was the third most important job in the country. While that sort of importance is undoubtedly exaggerated and untrue, the statement is a reflection of the prestige and high profile that goes with being the captain of the Indian cricket team.

There are few games where captains play as domineering a role as in cricket. In other team sports like hockey and football, captaincy is handed to the most outstanding or senior-most player. It a badge of honour and is worn only to pander to pride, for captains in these sports have precious little decisions to take. The coach is the strategist and it is he who decides who would be substituted, or play and in what position. If need be, the coach has the powers to even pull out the captain from the field.

However, in cricket the captain has a tremendous responsibility. The decisions he takes have a direct impact on the outcome of the match. He usually has a veto on the playing eleven. Thus, he is in the thick of things even before the match officially starts.

Indeed there have been times when captains have not had their way with the playing eleven. A good many cricket captains accept the selectors' diktats and try to build a cohesive unit with the resources given to them. Occasionally though, there comes a captain who is so peeved at not being given the team he wants that he goes out of the way to 'expose' the selectors' choice. The player concerned may not be given a bowl. Or he could be pressed into action deliberately at the wrong time and from the wrong end. Alternately, if he is a batsman he would pointedly be sent in to bat at the wrong time.

Of course, this bizarre manoeuvre is akin to cutting the nose to spite the face. But captains, particularly in India and Pakistan, have resorted to such tactics to cock-a-snook at the selectors. And Indian captains who have the support of the BCCI top brass usually get away with such peevishness.

Left-arm spinner Sunil Joshi who was at the receiving end in the Asia Cup in Dhaka in 2000 is well aware of this. He was given just two overs in the match against Sri Lanka—the 25th and 27th overs—by Skipper Saurav Ganguly. The rest of the bowlers were clobbered at will. But Joshi was shown as unwanted. Then he was sent in as number three even though he did not have the ability to bat that high against the new ball. It was obvious that the target of 277 and the new ball were far too stiff for him to handle.

Of course, Saurav has matured a lot since those days. But his motives continue to be viewed with suspicion.

Saurav took over the mantle from Sachin Tendulkar who, after dabbling in leadership for a while, decided that it was not his cup of tea. Tendulkar, for all his undoubted genius with the bat, simply failed to grow on the job as a captain. He could not convince the selectors on key issues. Worse, he could not shake off that Mumbai hang-up. On tours he was always in the company of Mumbai players. So much so the joke those days was that Tendulkar was unsure if he was leading India or Mumbai. Perhaps the fact that at least one senior player did not cooperate with him during those days made him fall back on players he knew, trusted and was comfortable with. Whatever the reasons, Tendulkar's stint as captain was eminently forgettable.

In this he suffered the same fate as other great players who made for poor captains—Ian Botham, Kapil Dev and, to a lesser extent, Viv Richards. Kapil Dev, at least, was successful at the World Cup in 1983. He led so much from the front and by instinct that whatever he dabbled in turned to gold in that memorable triumph. Kapil backed some of the average players to the hilt in that sojourn rather than batting maestro Sunil Gavaskar and Dilip Vengsarkar, and the move paid off splendidly. But whenever his chosen players failed to come good, Kapil himself batted and bowled like a true world beater.

This innate ability to play with a masterly touch and extricate the team from trouble is, nevertheless, seen as one of the impediments to these great players becoming good captains. They are so capable of performing near miracles with the bat and ball they simply cannot understand why lesser mortals fail to do the same. It is when they extend this logic to captaincy that they flop as leaders of the team.

Tendulkar, like Kapil and Botham before him, was a failure as captain because he simply could not understand the limitations of lesser players. But under Mohammed Azharuddin's leadership, Tendulkar, who was always in the thick of things when it came to on-field planning, had seemed like he could make all the right moves and take on the responsibility at any time. However, when elevated to the post of India's captain, a combination of factors ensured that Tendulkar lost out.

But in 1996, when he was handed the reins, the young 23-year-old Tendulkar seemed like he would lead India for a very, very long time. Rahul Dravid had just had a highly successful debut series in England and captaincy was far from his mind.

India played against Australia in a one-off Test in New Delhi and immediately after this the South African cricket team toured India to play a series of Tests and one-dayers. One of the warm-up matches that the South Africans played was a three-day match against the Ranji Trophy champions in Kochi. A whole lot of Karnataka players—Javagal Srinath, Venkatesh Prasad, Anil Kumble and Rahul—cried off from the match citing exhaustion as the reason. They had had a long tour of England followed by the one-off Test against Australia. The three-Test and five one-dayer series against South Africa was in the offing, to be quickly followed by two challenging tours to South Africa and West Indies.

Writing for *The Indian Express,* I had remarked that Rahul should not take the rest-route like the three bowlers as he was younger, had played lesser and was a purveyor of a different skill. If he felt fatigued he needed to just bat, get a few runs and not field. He was captaincy material and should seize every opportunity to drive that point home. By sitting out he would be sending wrong signals so early in his career (he had played just three Tests then), I had written. Subsequently, he was persuaded to play the game by the KSCA officials. But Rahul was annoyed by the article and was not to forget it.

After the series against South Africa at home, India toured South Africa. By now Rahul was one of the main stays of the batting. He underlined his immense potential with the superlative 148 and 81 in the final Test at Johannesburg. He literally tamed the fiery Allan Donald in that Test in one of the most memorable knocks by an Indian batsman.

India lost that series, but Rahul came away with his reputation greatly enhanced. He was seen as India's most complete batsman at this stage. The tour to West Indies followed. The Indian side was greatly handicapped by the loss of the services of Srinath very early in the tour. The fast bowler suffered a rotator cuff tear in his bowling arm and this virtually impoverished the new ball attack. It was left to the batsmen to salvage the series against a relatively weak West Indies team.

Rahul, with 360 runs in Tests, covered himself with glory. But the Indian batsmen collectively collapsed on a two-bounce Kensington Oval pitch at Barbados to lose the series.

During our sojourn at Barbados, the Barbados tourism promotion board and the Barbados Cricket Association organised a cruise for the players of both teams, media, umpires and officials. The five-deck ship was to go round the island of Barbados in a four-hour trip with drinks, dinner and entertainment thrown in.

The entire West Indies team was smartly turned out in fawn-coloured slacks and maroon T-shirts with the WICB logo and crest emblem standing out. The Indian team dressed easy. The cruise, loaded with numerous West Indies greats—Wes Hall, Joel Garner, Colin Croft, Desmond Haynes, Michael Holding, Lance Gibbs, Rohan Kanhai, et al.—the players, media, officials and the entertainment crew, waited on the docks till well past the time of departure. Most did not know why we were made to wait for an eternity, until a car pulled up dramatically and out climbed Brian Lara. He was the only West Indies cricketer who was not in the team's colours. Seeing him come late and not dressed in team uniform, many senior West Indies players loudly mouthed expletives.

As the cruise set off, all the dancing, drinking and partying was on the second tier. After a while, some of us broke away to explore the huge ship. It was then during a conversation on the top deck that Rahul opened up on the newspaper article and his nearly skipping the Kochi match against the South Africans.

"We'd been away from home for so long and there did not seem any point in playing that game. Also, I cannot understand why a

Karnataka match against a visiting side has to be played in Kochi," he stated.

I pointed out that he was the new hero of the side and everybody in the country wanted a glimpse of him and his batting. I then drew his attention to him being India captain material and that it was better that he got off on the right note with Board members and did all the right things at the start of his career.

But Rahul did not see things that way. "Sachin will lead for the next 10 years," he said. "Even otherwise, at this time of my career I am looking at perfecting my batting skills. Captaincy will be a distraction. May be later in my career I might consider it. But now I'm not even thinking about it."

Rahul was quite firm that he was not in the fray as far as leading India was concerned. I thought he would sooner, rather than later, change his mind.

Rahul had had a sound grounding when it came to leadership and captaincy, though in his early days in international cricket captaincy was far from his mind.

His school Principal Father Dennis Coelho praised his leadership skills from a very young age. He also stressed on his meticulous planning. "Rahul was the class monitor. Later, when he won the elections to become the captain of his house, Patricks, I was impressed with the amount of interest in took in the inter-house games and guided his house players. And it was not just cricket. He had already planned whom he wanted as the master in charge of the house and had sounded him out in advance. When he won the elections, the first thing he did was to meet the master and remind him of his commitment. I thought that was neat. Over the years I have seen him bring this meticulous planning into various aspects. I am sure he will one day be given the honour of leading India. He will bring a lot of dignity and honour to the job," said Coelho.

Rahul got his chance to lead India at a very young age. He led the Under-19 team against New Zealand Colts and did pretty well. "My only regret is that we did not play as much of under-19 cricket as youngsters do these days. In fact, when I played I was in my final year of under-19. Leading and playing a lot at that young age helps you hone your captaincy skills," said Rahul.

His first serious stint at captaincy at the first-class level came after he was overlooked for the 1996 World Cup team. He led Karnataka superbly right to the final. However, in the final, Anil Kumble, who had returned after the World Cup campaign, was asked to lead and he ensured the team won the championship.

Whatever disappointment Rahul had of not leading Karnataka to a Ranji Trophy title was overcome in 1998. That was the year the selectors messed with the one-day team, claiming they wanted to widen the player pool. Rahul was often kept out of the Indian one-day side under some pretext or the other. But Rahul made the situation work for him. He drove himself and his team with aims, goals and targets and used the opportunity to lead Karnataka to a superb title win.

"I rate it as one of the highlights of my career. I always wanted to lead the side to a Ranji Trophy triumph and had dreamt often of it. I cannot describe my joy when I held the Cup aloft that distant evening," recalled Rahul.

Rahul, though, had strong views on captaincy. "I never liked the idea of taking charge in the middle of the season. Whoever is appointed skipper must be put in charge for the entire season. If J Arunkumar is made Karnataka skipper, then he should stay the whole season, irrespective of who is going or coming. I have turned down leading in the middle of the season just for this reason. I believe that Arun knows the players' form and approach better as he has been with them throughout. Suddenly making me or Anil (Kumble) captain just because we return from international cricket is not fair or proper," he stressed.

Rahul, though, has never had such problems with leading India. Somehow, inadvertently he has been a stand-in captain again and again. His debut as India captain was hastened when Skipper Saurav Ganguly was penalised for on-field behaviour by Australian match Referee Barry Jarman. The latter believed that Saurav was putting unnecessary pressure on the umpires in the series against Zimbabwe and stated that his behaviour was bringing the game into disrepute. He threw him out of the final match, and this paved the way for Rahul to lead India for the first time.

India were already leading 4-0 and Rahul enjoyed himself in that tie at Rajkot. He was, obviously, delighted that he had met with success in his very first match as skipper.

Rahul's second match as India captain also came about with Saurav once again being docked a one-match suspension. This time, it was against Sri Lanka in Colombo and the match referee who disciplined him was West Indian Cammie Smith. Rahul made it a hat-trick of wins by leading India to victory against West Indies at Jodhpur. The only match he led and lost was the Vijayawada one-day international against the West Indies in the 2002-03 series

Rahul made his debut as Test captain against New Zealand in the Mohali Test in October, 2003. Saurav, this time, did not miss the match because of disciplining by the match referee, but owing to a surgery on a boil on his thigh. Rahul lost a crucial toss. The Kiwis made hay when the pitch was ideal for batting and notched up a massive 630 for six declared. When India batted, the pitch started deteriorating rapidly; but the Indian batsmen, particularly VVS Laxman, overcame the ignominy of a follow-on and battled out a draw.

With Saurav not recovering in time for the commencement of the three-nation One-day series between India, Australia and New Zealand, Rahul was asked to lead again.

Rahul, by all accounts, has the makings of a good captain. He is one of the top five batsmen in the world, is a very keen student of the game, is highly intelligent and has wonderful communication skills. The others in the team look up to him for inspiration. He is also not the one to put his foot in the mouth.

Expanding on the Indian government's proposal to resume cricketing contacts with Pakistan, Rahul, now the India captain, at least till Saurav recovers, was precise and politically correct: "There are people better qualified than me to take a stand on these matters. The government obviously knows a lot more than me on these things. I leave it to them. At the end of the day the country's interests should come first. If it is not in our interest to play them, then we should not. I have no view point on these things. I leave it to the government and the Board to decide what is best. If they say we should play, then that's fine by me. If they believe that the time is not right then we do not play. In case we play against them, I'd play them like any other team." That's Rahul—correct, flawless and to the point.

Certainly Rahul has a lot of things going for him. May be one day when the honour of leading the country on a major tour is thrust on him, his illustrious career will then have that complete look.

Chapter 16

One-day Winner

For Rahul the year 1998 was a traumatic one. The selectors and the team think-tank had set him up and led him to the chopping block. The schemers of Indian cricket had laid a trap, and an unsuspecting Rahul had walked into it. Their manipulations ensured that he was branded a 'not one-day' player and dropped from the side.

And what a record this 'not one-day' player has todate: An aggregate of 6,499 runs (at the start of the tri-series at home in 2003) from 190 innings (207 matches) with eight centuries, 44 fifties and an average of 39.15! Well, logically if a 'not one-day' player can have such a superb record then 'the one-day' players of the side must be veritable supermen! The question is: Are they?

Rahul's one-day career started innocuously enough. He did not do well in Singapore and UAE but the superb debut Test series in England gave him plenty of confidence in his ability to play at the highest level. By the time the Sahara Cup against Pakistan came along in Toronto, Rahul was in good nick. He was batting at number three and, against the Pakistani pacemen Wasim Akram and Waqar Younis, he came up with some fine scores: 39, 90, 46, 25 and 20. By all accounts Rahul had arrived as a batsman in this variety of the game also. The best, though, was yet to come.

That came in South Africa in the Standard Bank Tri-series final against an awesome South African attack comprising Allan Donald, Shaun Pollock, Klusner, Bryson, Kallis and Skipper Cronje. The Proteas had set 279 for a win from 50 overs and India seemed to be warming up to it when Sachin Tendulkar slammed a quick-fire 45. But rains and the consequent Duckworth and Lewis Rain Rule ensured that the target was suddenly made stiffer—to 251 from 40 overs. It was then that Rahul took the South African attack apart. Their highly rated pacemen had their reputation shred to pieces. Donald was left frothing and threatening to kill Rahul as he clobbered him. A superb six-over-long-on floored the 'white lightning'. Rahul, who had to suddenly step on the gas, made 84 with five fours and a six in 94 deliveries before he was fifth out at 210. The rest of the batsmen just caved in and India lost by mere 17 runs.

Rahul made three 50s in that series and followed it up with a superb 107 in a losing cause against Pakistan in the Independence Cup in Chennai.

But by now the plotters had their scheme in place. He was told that the team had a number of stroke-makers in Tendulkar, Azharuddin, Saurav Ganguly, Ajay Jadeja and others. He was asked to ensure that he kept his end going and played out 50 overs and left the scoring rate and acceleration to others.

This made Rahul excessively concentrate on preserving his wicket. His aim was to play out the overs in keeping with orders. Perhaps he got carried away by wicket preservation and did not rotate strike sufficiently. Perhaps he played into the hands of those who wanted to squeeze their favourites back into the playing eleven. Whatever, Rahul was suddenly confronted with statistics of his scoring rate and told that he did not fit in one-day cricket and was pushed out of the team.

It hurt like hell for a youngster who, for over two years, had been a regular member of the team. He had done everything right, including following orders, only to be made a sucker. Rahul was shattered and lost faith in those who were supposed to uphold the best interests of the team. He knew he had been robbed in broad daylight. But his background, education and culture would not allow him to speak out.

Even much, much later, the only things he would say are: "May be I needed to improve. May be there are lessons there for me to learn. May be when I am dropped next time I would know how to deal with it. I now know how to dig deep within myself and come up with answers."

Rahul, being the eternal gentleman, sought to play down the damage. "I was forced to improve. May be otherwise I would not have tried to improve. And in international cricket when people are always trying to sort you out that is dangerous."

Incredibly, when Rahul was dropped he was replaced not by better batsmen. Instead, the selectors fell back on Navjot Singh Sidhu who was clearly past his prime, Vinod Kambli whose international career, for all purposes was finished by Courtney Walsh's West Indies way back in 1994 and Hrishikesh Kanitkar who was neither a batsman nor a bowler at the international level.

With these being the quality of replacements, it was only a matter of time before sane elements in the selection committee restored Rahul to the national one-day side. Of course, the matter was wrenched out of their hands on international tours, particularly to Zimbabwe and later New Zealand where he was in sensational touch.

Rahul, who had made a century against Zimbabawe in the one-off Test in Harare, followed it up with a brilliant century in each innings (190 and 103) against New Zealand in the Hamilton Test. He took his great touch to the one-dayers and smashed an unbeaten 123 in Taupo. A string of good scores, including another century (116) against Sri Lanka in Nagpur, followed before he was accepted as an integral part of the one-day squad.

World Cup 1999

Rahul seemed to simply love the big stage. He had come into the tournament after a really tough year when he was unfairly dropped from the one-day side and was desperately keen to do well. He had prepared hard for the event and was further helped by the team going to England well in advance to get acclimatised.

The World Cups (in England and South Africa), with all the nations taking part and the entire cricketing world closely following it, seemed to get the best out of him. In 19 matches in World Cup, he had 779 runs including two centuries and five fifties for an average of 64.91. This was remarkable since his career average in one-day internationals (when this book was written, before the three-nation TVS Cup of 2003) was 39.15—well below his World Cup average.

In 1999, during the initial stages of the World Cup in England, the focus was on Sachin Tendulkar and Skipper Mohammed Azharuddin. Rahul, who not so long ago had been branded a 'not one-day player' was seen as someone whose batting technique would come in handy in seaming conditions. He would arrest any batting order collapse, said the cricket 'pundits'.

But by the time the event was over, it was Rahul who was hailed as the hero for the Indian team. The Indian challenge, in fact, threatened to go off-rails when they lost the first two matches to South Africa and Zimbabwe. The Indian Captain Azharuddin seemed to be aloof at most times, and the Manager, Anshuman Gaekwad seemed to be at a loss to rally the side. The team's Cricket Consultant, Australian Bobby Simpson, had joined the side in England and was working on strategies. But, with the batsmen failing at crucial times and the bowlers bowling far too many no-balls and wides, India looked a very poor cricketing side. To compound matter they were without the master batsman Tendulkar for the key tie against Zimbabwe. He had to fly back home following the untimely demise of his father.

Rahul made 54 from 75 deliveries in the match against South Africa and 13 against Zimbabwe. The Indian bowlers conceded 11 wides and 6 no balls against South Africa, and 21 wides, 16 no balls against Zimbabwe. Ajit Agarkar, for one, was awful, often spraying or overstepping when under pressure.

Yet, India could have pulled it off against Zimbabwe, except that the batsmen developed cold feet and threw away the match in one Henry Olanga over. The fast bowler had bowled all over the place till then. But with India needing seven runs from six overs he produced the magical spell to get three wickets for three runs to help defeat a shell-shocked India by a mere three runs.

By now the rumbling in distant India could be heard in England. Thousands of Indians had flown down for the tournament. In fact, the who's who of corporate India, filmdom, entertainment industry, politicians, bureaucrats and media were all in England following the fortunes of the team. This apart, a whole lot of salesmen, cable operators and other Indians who had won a trip to the World Cup as part of sales incentives were also around. If anything, all these fans only added to the pressure.

In such a must-win scenario, Rahul flowered in the next few matches to keep the tri-colour flying. He blasted an unbeaten 104 in 109 deliveries and added 237 blistering runs in only 29 overs with Tendulkar (140 n.o. in 101 balls). The latter returned in time for the game against Kenya and his presence lifted the spirits of the team and the Indian fans.

India, thus, notched up their first points in the World Cup. The next game against Sri Lanka was even more crucial, for the Lankans were the World Cup champions. They had a number of very good players in Arjuna Ranatunga, Aravinda De Silva, Sanath Jayasuriya, Marvan Attapattu, Chaminda Vaas, Muthiah Muralitharan, among others. India simply had to win this match if they had to have a chance of making the Super Six.

Once again Rahul came good. He and Saurav Ganguly put on the first 300-run partnership in one-day internationals. They added a whopping 318 runs for the second wicket with Saurav making a grand 183 (158 balls, 17 fours and seven sixes) and Rahul being just as impressive in his knock of 145 (129 balls, 17 fours and one six). India made 373 for six and simply cantered home. Rahul also kept wickets in this match. In the previous game he had taken over from an injured Nayan Mongia after the ninth over, so had virtually kept in two matches in succession.

By now all Indian matches were drawing capacity crowds. The match against hosts England in Edgbaston triggered off a debate in the English media: Should watching be confined to the wine-sipping, 'polite', gentle applauding, over-dressed spectators, or the vociferous, drums-banging, trumpet-blowing, flag-waving, with T-shirts and shorts sporting emotional fans?

Actually, nobody cared for these silly debates, for when the match commenced, England might as well have been playing in Eden Gardens or one of the Indian stadia. The colourful Indian fans had packed the stadium and flowed all over the streets outside it. They ensured that the match remained a cricket carnival and boosted the morale of the Indian team.

Batting on the Edgbaston pitch was not easy. The ball seamed quite a bit. The pacemen were also getting the ball to swing. Under the circumstances, Rahul's top score of 53 in 82 deliveries was worth its weight in gold. The second highest score was 40 by Saurav while Ajay Jadeja made 39. Rahul's watchful vigil, though, helped India to 232.

It was apparent even then that if the Indian pacemen bowled on a length, England would struggle under these conditions. Debashish Mohanty, who was preferred to Agarkar, Venkatesh Prasad, Javagal

Srinath and Saurav did just that. England were bundled out for 169 and a joyful India squeezed into the Super Six.

It was the format of the Super Six which defeated India in that World Cup. They had lost in the league phase to the other two teams that made the grade from their group (South Africa and Zimbabwe) and hence had no points to carry into the Super Six phase. This meant that India would have to defeat all the three qualifiers from the other group, Australia, Pakistan and New Zealand, to get six points, while South Africa, who made the grade by carrying forward four points, needed just one win against one of the three teams to be on par with India. It was a bizarre format alright.

India lost to Australia in the first Super Six encounter. Rahul made 2, Sachin zero and Saurav 8. However, there was still the match against Pakistan to look forward to.

The English media hyped up this match to fever pitch and claimed that there would be blood on the streets if the fans of these two rival nations were not separated by iron fences, moat and the like. They had probably watched too much football where their home-grown hooligans, after guzzling barrels of liquor, constantly mistook the rival fans' heads for a football.

Sure the Old Trafford ground was awash with a riot of colours. But they were all Indian and Pakistani colours. The Pakistani green was nearly as predominant as the Indian tri-colour and blue (team colours). The noise level at the stadium that day was amazing. But this, once again, was true carnival spirit—the very spirit the World Cup hoped to capture.

In the match, Rahul again top-scored with 61 off 89 deliveries. Saurav had pulled out of the match complaining of a bad knee. But Azharuddin chipped in with a useful 59 and Sachin with 45. The boastful Shoaib Akhtar, who on the eve of the match had talked non-stop of what he would do to the Indian batsmen, went for 55 runs from 10 overs on a bowler-friendly pitch.

When Pakistan batted, Saeed Anwar seemed to be in good nick. But the tall paceman Venkatesh Prasad was simply brilliant. He bowled like a maestro and bagged five wickets for just 27 runs while Srinath (3 for 37) and Anil Kumble (2 for 43) were just as impressive. Pakistan were bundled out for 180 and thereby lost by 47 runs. It was a fantastic win for India and made up for the earlier disappointments in the tournament. Once again in a bowler-friendly, crucial match, it was Rahul who had carried the Indian batting on his shoulder.

In the next game, even before India took the field against New Zealand, they knew they were out of the tournament. The team, thus, did not have its heart in an inconsequential match and lost.

For Rahul it proved to be a very good World Cup. He had scored two centuries, batted with plenty of poise and kept wickets with great enthusiasm whenever asked to. The only sour point was when he stayed back and did a bit of television commentary and ended up getting a show-cause notice for it from the BCCI.

"It was a great experience sharing the commentary box with Richie Benaud, Sunil Gavaskar, Ravi Shastri and Imran Khan and watching a World Cup final from the media box in Lord's. I was a bit surprised when I got the letter from BCCI. But it was more like a caution. They said I had to take their permission before giving commentary," said Rahul with a big smile on his face.

World Cup 2003

By the time the World Cup in South Africa commenced, Rahul was firmly entrenched in the Indian team. The fact that he was also keeping wickets added another dimension to his play and considerably fortified the side's batting. It permitted Skipper Saurav to call up an extra batsman and strengthen the side.

For whatever the pundits said about the bowling, it was the Indian team's indifferent batting in crunch situations that had betrayed it time and again. The much-vaunted batting seldom stood up to pressure and it was only after India added another batsman to their line-up did they really start looking the part.

The additional batsman in this case turned out to be Mohammed Kaif. With him in the line-up, the Indian batting order read: Sachin, Virender Sehwag, Dinesh Mongia, Saurav, Rahul, Yuvaraj, Kaif, Kumble or Harbhajan, Zaheer Khan, Srinath and Aashish Nehra.

This ensured that there was plenty of batting muscle around. The Indians put this to the test successfully in England in the months preceding the South Africa World Cup. In the Lord's match, England had made a huge total of 271. If ever India needed its batting order to come good, this was the time. Sehwag and Saurav put on 109 runs for the first wicket. But after Sehwag (71) departed, India lost Mongia (1), Sachin (1) and Saurav (43) in quick succession to slip to 141 for four. With more than half the overs and the cream of the batting gone, India were in trouble.

It was then that Rahul (73 n.o.) and Yuvaraj (64 n.o.) got stuck in a superb partnership to see the side home.

India, with many wins and some defeats between then and the World Cup, was hoping to cash in on the batting depth in South Africa. Rahul keeping wickets was central to this strategy.

But before the World Cup started the Indian players were drawn into an unsavoury controversy. The Board of Control for Cricket in India and the ICC had got into a public spat over Imaging Rights and Ambush Marketing clauses in their agreement. The Indian players who had entered into legal contracts with sponsors were asked to keep those contracts in suspension for a six-month duration before, during and after the World Cup. This was to ensure that the ICC's sponsors could use images of the players and also pre-empt any ambush marketing by rival sponsors.

The players held that their future earnings were being compromised and they were being forced to violate their existing agreements. The Board claimed that it had the best interests of the players in mind and that the ICC had introduced certain clauses into the agreement after the signing. The ICC flatly denied it, saying the Board was aware of the clauses when it signed and would have to pay damages if the Indian players violated the clauses. Reams of newsprint and hours of television chat were expended on this contracts issue. At one stage it looked like the main Indian players would be dropped from the team. Rahul, Sachin and Saurav, the big three who had the cream of the sponsorship contracts, stood to lose a lot. Ultimately some sort of a compromise was reached and the World Cup went ahead. Incidentally, close to a year after the event the Board is still to receive US$ 9 million from the ICC.

In South Africa, at the World Cup campaign, things almost went awry from the beginning as the much-vaunted Indian batting depth got a rude jolt in the initial two matches. India were dismissed for 204 by lowly Holland in the first match, but pulled off a win through the bowling of Srinath and Kumble. The next match, though, was a disaster. The Australian pacemen bundled out India for 125 at the Centurion and won by nine wickets.

Like in England four years ago, doubts were once again raised about India's ability to raise the level of the game. Many in the media stated that the Indian team was suffering the effects of a burnout. They had been playing non-stop cricket for 12 months now and were too exhausted coming into the World Cup, said the pundits.

The match against Zimbabwe, India's third in the tournament, was touted as a grudge game. It worked wonders for the team. Sachin (81) and Rahul (43 n.o.) held the batting together and laid the foundation for an easy 83-run win.

India slaughtered Namibia next before running into old foe England at Kingsmead. The pitch, supposedly the quickest in South Africa, worked to the Indians' advantage. Rahul (62) and Sachin (50) piloted the team to a healthy 250 for nine and, with Aashish Nehra (6 for 23) bowling the spell of his life, England were shot out for 168.

The team was by now working like a well-oiled machine. Gone was all talk of burnout. Winning produced its own momentum and the players were raring to go. Bitter rivals Pakistan were next in the fray and everybody knew this was going to be the match of the tournament.

The left-handed Saeed Anwar batted splendidly for Pakistan and guided them to an impressive 273 for seven at the Centurion. Although India could have made the Super Sixes stage even without winning this game, it would have been a bitter progress if they had lost to Pakistan. The Pakistani fans and players, though, were already in celebration mood when their innings ended. They thought with that huge total of theirs and their famed bowling attack they simply could not lose from here. But within a couple of overs of the commencement of the Indian innings, or more appropriately Sachin's innings, the Pakistanis were a mute lot.

Sachin reserved his best for the Pakistani chatterbox Shoaib Akhtar. He smashed the living daylights out of him in just two overs and brazenly took the battle into the Pakistani camp. With Mohammed Kaif (35), Rahul (44 n.o.) and Yuvaraj (50 n.o.) rallying around splendidly, Sachin's magnificent knock of 98 ensured that India successfully chased Pakistan's huge total.

After this, the three Super Sixes matches against Kenya, Sri Lanka and New Zealand were a breeze. Rahul made 32 against Kenya and an unbeaten 52 against New Zealand. The semi-final against Kenya was again one-sided. Saurav (111 n.o.), Sachin (83) and Sehwag (33) had clobbered the African outfit into submission. India were thus into the final of the World Cup. The last time they had come this far was 20 years ago when they won the championship. Could they pull it off again?

All roads led to the Wanderers Stadium in Johannesburg that day. Just getting to the stadium was a major chore. There were street protests galore against the American invasion of Iraq. Cars and taxis were stopped a fair distance from the stadium. Spectators were asked to walk the rest of the way. Metal detectors, security personnel and sniffer dogs were all over. So were some of the most gorgeous women, marvelously dressed and part of one big street carnival.

The atmosphere was truly festive. The only thing missing was firecrackers. Those pyrotechnics was provided in the batting crease by Aussie Skipper Ricky Ponting. Openers Adam Gilchrist and Mathew Hayden had set the tone with a 105-run stand in just 14 overs. But that paled into insignificance when Ponting got going. The right-hander took his time settling down. After that it was sheer mayhem. He clobbered Zaheer, Srinath, Nehra, Harbhajan and the part-timers in one of the most destructive pieces of batsmanship in the World Cup.

Ponting smashed eight sixes and four boundaries in a 121-ball effort worth an unbeaten 140. Damien Martyn made an unbeaten 88 and the Aussies galloped their way to an unbeatable 359 for two in 50 overs.

In the Indian reply, Sehwag made 82 and Rahul 47, but it was in a lost cause. For a while Indian supporters rejoiced when a sudden cloudburst halted play. Although 25 overs were still to be completed, India needed just a few runs to stay ahead of the required run-rate as per the Duckworth-Lewis system that would come into force in case the match was subsequently called off. If 25 overs could not be bowled that day, then the final would have been replayed the following day. However, the suspense lasted for just an hour or so. The rains cleared, the ground was quickly dried and the match was continued till India were bundled out for 234.

The Indian team had come much further in this tournament than its supporters had expected. So the usual brickbats that accompanied Indian defeats were absent.

Rahul had a decent tournament. He was not as prolific as he was in England, but had done sufficiently well both with the bat and behind the stumps to enhance his reputation as a top-notch player. Once again the middle order depended on him to provide the stability and he seldom let the team down. For all the barbs he had attracted in 1998, he was now seen as a key member of the one-day squad. Rahul claimed after the World Cup that he had had his fill of wicketkeeping and would not pick up the gloves again. Now that remains to be seen.

Chapter 17

The Ideal Professional

Only a few Indian batsmen have been successful in English County Cricket. The daily grind that calls for constant travel, playing matches five to six days a week, eating different food, playing in cold and windy conditions and a whole lot of other chores that go into being a professional cricketer seems to have defeated quite a few Indian batsmen.

The bowlers, Anil Kumble, Javagal Srinath, Bishen Bedi, Dilip Doshi and S Venkataraghavan, adapted to the needs of county cricket and performed far more successfully than Indian batsmen. Of course, batsmen of a different era like Ranjit Singhji, Duleep Singhji, the two Nawabs of Pataudi, Farook Engineer, et al. met with a lot of success.

However, batsmen of more recent vintage, Sunil Gavaskar, Mohammed Azharuddin, a young Sachin Tendulkar, Mohammed Kaif, Saurav Ganguly, Virender Sehwag and Yuvaraj Singh, to name a few, did not have as much success in county cricket as they had in international cricket. Somehow they did not find the inspiration to lift their game in county cricket. Of course, most of them scored big figures of runs against world-class attacks when turning out for India. Yet, for all their proven record in international cricket, their county track record in comparison is quite dismal.

In such a scenario, Rahul, in contrast has been a standout, both for Kent in his debut year in 2000 and for Scotland in 2003. "Very few Indian batsmen of late have been a hit with county sides. But Rahul was fantastic when he played for us," said Mini Patel, Kent's left arm spinner who had toured India with the England A team in 1994.

Rahul, in 16 matches for Kent that year, scored 1221 runs with two centuries and eight 50s for an average of 55.50.

John Wright, the former New Zealand Test opener and current coach of the Indian team, was the Kent County Club coach when Rahul played. "He had come to New Zealand the previous year. I was very impressed with the way he played there. He was the top batsman in that series, with a century in each innings in the Hamilton Test. Rahul spoke to me and said that he would like to come over for a stint in county cricket to sharpen his skills.

"I knew he would be the ideal overseas professional. When we scout for players we not only look for a good player, but also for someone who is a quality person and can be a good leader off the field. It is important that the pro sets a good example, not only from a performance point of view but also by the way he practises, approaches a game and carries himself. Kent had a number of good young players and the presence of a cricketer of Rahul's stature and ability to communicate and inspire would have been excellent for these young English professionals. So when an opportunity arose, we signed him up."

Kent's overseas player the year 1999 had been the Australian all-rounder Andrew Symonds. By nature he was boisterous in the dressing room. Rahul, on the other hand, was quieter and more serious. In this he was much like the Sri Lankan batsman Aravinda Desilva who had been such a hit with Kent in the early 90s.

"I was very keen to play county cricket. I knew that a season there would have helped my game immensely. County cricket is like a sort of finishing school. I wanted to taste it. And so when I got this offer from Kent I took it up," said Rahul.

"The best thing I liked about Rahul was that he was not coming to make a fat pay-packet. He was very hungry to experience the English county season and genuinely wanted to become a better player. Usually the Australians are the first preference as they are so tough and their cricket season does not clash with the English season.

"Then there is the difference in culture. In Kent we wanted a professional who could fit in. We wanted somebody who would be popular around the county club with the players, members, supporters and fans. It had to be somebody who also spoke well to the 17- and 18-year-olds of Kent County Club. Besides these he had to be a very good player. Rahul had the focus and the mental and physical toughness to be a day-in-and-day-out player. Everybody at Kent was proud of him and would certainly have him over anytime he chose to come and play," said Wright.

When Rahul walked into the Kent dressing room he was immediately accepted. Kent was led by Mathew Fleming whose family owned the Fleming Banking group. Fleming had a good education and was, in fact, related to Ian Fleming of James Bond fame. He was a strong leader. He had played for England in a few one-day internationals and was a batsman and medium pacer of some ability. There were a number of young batters on the staff in Robert Key, who subsequently played a few games for England, Mathew Walker and David Fulton. They benefited enormously from Rahul's work ethics.

"He was a stickler for nets. As soon as he came over he wanted to practise. He wanted to do it all the time. At other times he would be working out in the gym. The players loved his attitude. He was such a positive influence on them," said Mini Patel.

Rahul's love for batting came to the fore in the matches. The Kent players marvelled at the way he handled pressure. He would bat on, battling the bowlers and conditions. He was moved around in the batting order so that the team could get the maximum from him. He even opened in some of the one-dayers. More than anything, the club supporters and players liked the way he valued his wicket and never threw it away.

The best of his innings came against Hampshire, for whom Shane Warne was the overseas professional. It was an away game at Portsmouth and billed as a clash between the world's best spinner and the world's top batsman. The build up for the match went on for days together and this attracted a huge crowd.

"The pitch took quite a bit of turn. It was ideal for a bowler of Warne's ability and class. But Rahul on the day was simply fantastic. I think he just fed on the pressure and expectations and played one of the most brilliant innings I've seen. In fact, all the Kent players dropped whatever they were doing and watched the battle intensely. Robert Key who was the non-striker in the century partnership for the second wicket saw the way Rahul dominated Warne that day and could not stop talking about it," said Mini Patel.

Recalling the match, the Kent coach Wright said that he spoke after the game to the English Umpire John Hampshire. "He said, 'here I am watching a county game on a very fine day where Shane Warne is bowling and Rahul Dravid is batting. I have never seen Warne get blasted in such a fashion by anyone. Rahul's batting is simply amazing'."

Rahul made 137 in that match. But more than the number of runs it was the manner in which he made them, and handled pressure and the Warne factor that thrilled the supporters of Kent.

In fact, Rahul's only problems that season seemed to be with the sponsored car and his driving. "We all used to heave a sigh of relief whenever we saw Rahul pull into the parking lot," said Wright. It was an understatement for the Indian batsman never really came to terms with driving on the motorway that year.

"Usually Rahul and I travelled together," said Mini Patel. "I stayed near London and it was easy to drive everywhere from there as all the motorways link London. Once he had said he would come home by mid-day and we'd drive together for the match. But there was no sign of him. By 1 p.m. I panicked. But I could not reach him on his cell phone. Then at 1.30 p.m. he called up to say that he was with the police and somewhere near Sussex. He had lost his way and had overshot London. He was stopped and fined by the police for using a cell phone while driving. Luckily for us we were travelling the day before the match!"

Rahul's adventures with the car and police did not end there. He and Wright had driven to Manchester and pulled in at the club. "He did not know where to park. I pointed out a spot. But when we came back, the car was gone. Here we were, the club's overseas pro and the coach walking around at 10 p.m. searching for the car! It had been towed away for being parked in a No-Parking zone. It was really funny," recalled Wright.

"Rahul was thoroughly confused by all the loops and exits on the motorway. The other guys were scared to travel with him because of this. I was voted as the person who would drive him around," said Mini Patel.

By all accounts Rahul had improved this aspect of his life when he headed for another stint in the National Cricket League in the United

Kingdom in 2003. He had just married Dr Vijeeta Pendarkar and used the season with Scotland as a honeymoon-cum-working trip. He played only the one-dayers for Scotland as he wanted an easy schedule. Rahul, and the Indian team, had had a hectic schedule till the conclusion of the World Cup in South Africa. He was therefore looking forward to an atmosphere where he could relax and also play the game.

Scotland's soothing environment did much to rejuvenate him. He and his wife enjoyed the pleasures of beautiful Scotland. The well-spaced-out one-day schedule also helped him keep in touch with the game. Like he had with Kent, Rahul became an asset in the dressing room, especially as Scotland sought experience to help them earn a berth in the 2007 World Cup. But his hunger for the game and its intricacies never waned. He attended a coaching course for coaches conducted by Bob Woolmer in Scotland, mingled freely and participated enthusiastically, seeking answers to queries.

Playing in just the one-dayers for Scotland, Rahul met with immense success as his record proves: 11 matches, an aggregate of 600 runs inclusive of three centuries and two 50s. His highest was an unbeaten 129 against Nottinghamshire. He also made an unbeaten 120 against Somerset and 114 in 102 deliveries against Northamptonshire. Rahul topped the batting averages at 66.66 and a strike rate of 92.73.

Rahul loved his season with Scotland so much that if the BCCI to whom he is contracted permit him, he would be back for the 2004 season also.

Chapter 18

To be Continued...

Father Dennis Coelho, Principal of St Joseph's Boys School, did not know how prophetic he could be when he spoke to Rahul and his parents long, long ago, when Rahul was still in his early teens. On that distant day, when Rahul and his parents apologetically approached him and hesitatingly sought permission for Rahul to miss a few days of school and instead play for Karnataka in the Under-15 tournament in Vijayawada, he said, "It is a great adventure he is embarking on. Let's support him."

Now, after scores of Tests, hundreds of one-day internationals and thousands of miles of travel, Rahul's adventure is far from over.

There are more Tests, ODIs and centuries in the offing. And may be there is even a bit of wicketkeeping to be done before he can move on to other things. So what is the road ahead for this excellent cricketer, diligent academic and gentleman extraordinaire?

The immediate priority would be to do well in the series against Australia in Australia in late 2003 and early 2004. Rahul has met with success all over the world, but on his lone tour to Australia during the 1999-2000 season he did not have too many happy memories. He is immensely hungry for success in Australia for he knows that if he is to be accepted as all-time great he needs acceptance in Australia too.

The Australians will come at him with everything they have. They know that he is the batsman who will anchor the middle order.

"Australia is the big thing for Rahul. If he is able to get runs there, then he would have batted well everywhere," said the Indian Coach John Wright. "When Rahul does well, India do well. There is no doubt about that. Obviously, Tendulkar is Tendulkar. But in all conditions Rahul is the man," he stressed.

Immediately after the Australian tour there is the challenging tour to Pakistan. The government has cleared it as of October 2003 as a part of the confidence-building measure. But as far as Indo-Pak relations are concerned, till the tour is done and over with, nothing can be said for certain. Rahul has never played in Pakistan and it would be a big challenge for him to take on the Pakistanis in their backyard. He certainly would revel in that. Rahul, being a meticulous planner, would be well prepared for both the tours.

The planning Rahul brings into almost everything he does is uncanny. Even where his marriage was concerned, he ensured that it was at the end of the cricket season and would not distract him from playing cricket during the season. He was so meticulous and systematic that he planned to stay in the game in the months following the wedding and signed a contract to play for Scotland in the relatively less intense second division. He spaced out his playing schedule in such a manner that he was required to play just 11 matches in three-and-a-half months. In this way he enjoyed his honeymoon and also took in a bit of competitive cricket. At the same time, far from the fish-bowl syndrome that dogs top cricketers in India, he initiated Vijeeta into the life, work ethics and culture of an international cricketer. So the marriage, honeymoon and cricketing season with Scotland all worked out to perfection for Rahul.

The marriage itself was an arranged one. Rahul, whose younger brother Vijay got married in 2001, and Vijeeta's families knew each other from decades, even before Rahul and Vijeeta were born.

Sharad and Pusha, Rahul's parents, moved to Bangalore after their marriage in 1967. Sharad was employed in Kissan, Bangalore, at that time and Pushpa joined him after the wedding. Meanwhile, the Pendarkars, Maharashtrian couple from Nagpur, had also relocated to Bangalore. Vijeeta's father was with the Indian Air Force and had been posted in Bangalore. Her mother, incidentally, was the elder sister of former Indian shuttle player Pradeep Gandhe. The young couples, Dravids and the Pendarkars, used to visit each other in Bangalore, long before either Rahul or Vijeeta was born.

Subsequently, the Dravids used to visit the Pendarkars when the latter were posted elsewhere and thereby kept in constant touch. When Pushpa had her art exhibition at the Jehangir Art Gallery in Mumbai, the Dravids stayed with the Pendarkars. They used to visit them often in Nagpur too. Later, whenever Rahul played in Nagpur he would visit the Pendarkars.

"It was only as a family friend," pointed out Sharad about his son paying visits to Vijeeta's home. Pushpa, who was keen that Rahul got married as early as possible, believed that Vijeeta and Rahul would make an ideal match. The Dravids and the Pendarkars got together and thus arranged the marriage.

The news of the marriage caused a stir. Rahul had not spoken about it even to his closest friends. It was only after the invitations started going out that they became aware of it. Rahul wanted to keep it a solemn and private affair, and not convert it into a media circus with the whole of Bangalore barging in and making it a *mela*. The newspapers soon got wind of it and for days there was speculation whether the wedding would be in Bangalore or Nagpur. Some of the mediamen tapped into their sources in the five-star hotels to find out when and where the marriage ceremony would take place. But they drew a blank. Some pried news out of Rahul's neighbours. Others took to tracking Vijeeta and her parents.

Vijeeta tried to slip into Bangalore by taking the train from Nagpur. But somebody had tipped off the media and there was a huge contingent of photographers and mediamen among the entourage that greeted her. Finally, the marriage was held at the Air Force Station in the outskirts of Bangalore. The attendant military security ensured that prying eyes were kept away. Rahul and Vijeeta came down to a city hotel to pose for the media photographers and a reception.

Most of Rahul's teachers, friends and all those who had played cricket at any level with him were invited to the wedding. "It is a reflection of the regard and esteem his teachers have for him that so many are here today," said Fr. Coelho at the reception. Shortly, after another reception at Nagpur, the newly-wed couple left for Scotland.

Vijeeta, who has completed her masters in surgery in Nagpur, is currently practicing at the prestigious St John's Hospital in Bangalore. Rahul too has some unfinished business to catch up with. He excelled in academics and did just one year of business management with the Bangalore University before the demands of international cricket forced him to put his pursuit of academics in cold storage. His long-term ambition is to complete his business management from the prestigious London School of Economics. But for the moment that will have to wait. There are a lot more battles to be fought and won on the cricket front before he embarks on a career after cricket.

Career Statistics

Rahul Dravid

Born on 11 January, 1973 at Indore.

Plays for Karnataka. Also played for Kent in 2000 and for Scotland in 2003 in English County.

Right-hand batsman, off-break bowler. Has been a makeshift wicketkeeper for India in one-day international matches.

Ranji Trophy Debut: *vs. Maharashtra at Pune on 2 February, 1991 at the age of 18 years and 21 days.*

Test Debut: *vs. England at Lord's on 20 June, 1996 at the age of 23 years and 5 months.*

One-Day International Debut: *vs. Sri Lanka at Singapore on 3 April, 1996 at the age of 23 years and 2 months.*

Facts and Figures

In	*Mts*	*Inns*	*No*	*Runs*	*HS*	*Avge*	*100s*	*50s*	*Cts*
Ranji Trophy	37	52	7	3638	215	80.84	14	17	43
Duleep Trophy	16	27	3	1069	188	44.54	3	6	13
Irani Trophy	2	4	1	294	132*	98.00	1	1	3
Tests	71	122	13	5927	222	54.37	15	29	90
Against Visiting Teams	11	17	2	628	145*	41.87	1	5	11
In Tour Matches	26	41	12	153	137	53.21	3	10	23/1
For Kent in 2000	16	25	3	1221	182	55.50	2	8	15
In Limited Over Matches									
Subbaiah Pillai	8	7	2	444	130	88.80	1	2	1
Deodhar	12	11	1	335	79	33.50	0	4	7/2
Wills	3	3	1	76	36	38.00	0	0	0
Challenger	19	17	1	829	107	51.81	1	8	8
One-day Internationals	207	190	24	6499	153	39.15	8	44	125/10

In Ranji Trophy (for Karnataka)

In	*Mts*	*Inns*	*No*	*Runs*	*HS*	*Avge*	*100s*	*50s*	*Cts*
1990-91	2	2	0	216	134	108.00	1	1	0
1991-92	5	7	1	380	128	63.33	2	1	13
1992-93	6	9	2	586	200*	83.71	1	5	3
1993-94	7	11	3	644	151*	80.50	2	4	10
1994-95	1	1	0	191	191	191.00	1	0	0
1995-96	6	8	0	460	153	57.50	3	0	7
1997-98	8	11	1	731	215	73.10	2	4	4
1998-99	1	1	0	210	210	210.00	1	0	2
1999-2000	1	2	0	220	149	110.00	1	1	4
Total	**37**	**52**	**7**	**3638**	**215**	**80.84**	**14**	**17**	**43**

Against Each State

Against	*Mts*	*Inns*	*No*	*Runs*	*HS*	*Avge*	*100s*	*50s*	*Cts*
Andhra	4	5	2	530	200	176.66	2	2	3
Assam	1	1	0	38	38	38.00	0	0	0
Baroda	1	1	0	9	9	9.00	0	0	2
Bengal	2	2	0	143	134	71.50	1	0	3
Goa	5	5	0	318	126	63.60	2	1	9
Hyderabad	7	11	0	737	210	67.00	2	4	5
Kerala	4	5	2	341	128	113.66	2	1	7
Maharashtra	1	1	0	82	82	82.00	0	1	0
Madhya Pradesh	1	2	0	96	89	48.00	0	1	0
Mumbai	1	2	0	116	69	58.00	0	1	2
Orissa	1	1	0	138	138	138.00	1	0	0
Punjab	1	2	0	93	55	46.50	0	1	1
Rajasthan	1	2	0	220	149	110.00	1	1	4
Railways	1	2	1	77	65	77.00	0	1	2
Tamil Nadu	5	9	2	485	151*	69.28	2	2	3
Uttar Pradesh	1	1	0	215	215	215.00	1	0	1
Total	**37**	**52**	**7**	**3638**	**215**	**80.84**	**14**	**16**	**42**

Innings by Innings in Ranji Trophy

No.	Season	Against	Venue		Runs	Result
1.	1990-91	Maharashtra	Pune	ct. AP Deshapande b Y Kadam	82	Drawn
2.		Bengal	Kolkata	ct. Arun Lal b S Sensharma	134	Drawn
3.	1991-92	Goa	KGF	b A Shetty	126	Won by 10 wkts
4.		Kerala	Bijapur	ct. KG Jayakumar b KNA Padmanaban	128	Won by inns & 242 runs
5.		Andhra	Vishakapatnam	ct. Vinay Kumar b Reddy, DS	29	Won by inns & 74 runs
6.		Hyderabad	Secunderabad	b Abrar Ahmed	15	Drawn
				bowled Arshad Ayub	21	
7.		Tamil Nadu	Bhadravathi	not out	61	Won by 1 wkt
				ct. Sanjay b Subramaniam	0	
8.	1992-93	Goa	Panaji	ct. Cardozo b A Shetty	54	Won by inns & 73 runs
9.		Kerala	Kozhikode	b Ramprakash	37	Won by inns & 74 runs
10.		Andhra	Bangalore	not out	200	
				not out	56	Drawn
11.		Hyderabad	Hubli	ct. Ramesh Kumar b Swaroop	55	Drawn
12.		Tamil Nadu	Chennai	ct. Robin Singh b Venkataramana	79	Lost by 6 wkts
				ct. Sharath b Subramaniam	9	
13.		Madhya Pradesh	Bangalore	ct. Patel b Lahore	89	Lost by 5 runs
				ct. Zuber Khan b Hirwani	7	
14.	1993-94	Andhra	Vijayawada	lbw b Ramkishen	54	Drawn

No.	Season	Against	Venue		Runs	Result
15.		Hyderabad	Secunderabad	ct. Sridhar b Arshad Ayub	60	Lost by 8 wkts
				bowled VP Raju	19	
16.		Goa	Bangalore	st. Cardoza b R Kambli	8	Won by inns & 85 runs
17.		Tamil Nadu	Bangalore	ct. Vasu b Gokulkrishnan	37	Won by 131 runs
				not out	151	
18.		Kerala	Bangalore	not out	105	Won by 8 wkts
				not out	56	
19.		Assam	Bangalore	ct. Das b Chakraborthy	38	Won by inns & 186 runs
20.		Mumbai	Bangalore	ct. Dighe b Patel	47	Drawn
				ct. Shastri b Patel	69	
21.	1994-95	Andhra	Bangalore	c & b Prakash	191	Won by inns & 79 runs
22.	1995-96	Goa	Bangalore	ct. Kuchelkar b SV Mudkavi	108	Won by inns & 237 runs
23.*		Tamil Nadu	Bhadravathi	ct. Robin Singh b Subramaniam	13	Drawn
24.*		Bengal	Bangalore	ct. Saba Karim b C Sharma	9	Won by inns & 29 runs
25.*		Baroda	Bangalore	st. More b Buch	9	Won by inns & 79 runs
26.*		Hyderabad	Bangalore	run out	153	Drawn
				lbw b Kanwaljit Singh	33	
27.		Tamil Nadu	Chennai	ct. Ramesh b Vasu	114	Drawn
				bowled Vasu	21	
28.	1997-98	Kerala	Bangalore	b P Manoj	15	Won by inns & 23 runs
29.		Goa	Bangalore	b Suresh	22	Won by 10 wkts

No.	*Season*	*Against*	*Venue*		*Runs*	*Result*
30.		Hyderabad	Secunderabad	run out	99	Drawn
31.		Punjab	Bangalore	ct. D Mongia b Harvinder Singh	38	Won by 262 runs
				ct. Mehra b Harvinder Singh	55	
32.		Railways	Bangalore	b Parida	65	Won by 6 wkts
			not out	12		
33.		Orissa	Rourkela	ct. Das b Jayachandra	138	Won by Inns & 123 runs
34.*		Hyderabad	Secunderabad	ct. Nanda Kishore b Manohar	71	Won by 1 wkt
				lbw b Kanwaljit Singh	1	
35.*		Uttar Pradesh	Bangalore	run out	215	Drawn
36.*	1998-99	Hyderabad	Bangalore	ct. Vanka Pratap b Vishnu Vardhan	210	Won by Inns & 3 runs
37.	1999-00	Rajasthan	Bangalore	bowled R Kanwat	71	Won by 139 runs
				bowled Anup Dave	149	

* Captain.

In Duleep Trophy (for South Zone)

Season	*Mts*	*Inns*	*No*	*Runs*	*HS*	*Avge*	*100s*	*50s*	*Cts*
1991-92	2	3	0	54	29	18.00	0	0	0
1992-93	1	2	0	14	14	7.00	0	0	0
1993-94	4	7	1	80	23*	13.33	0	0	7
1994-95	3	6	0	314	148	52.33	1	2	0
1995-96	4	6	2	353	101*	88.25	1	3	4
2000-2001	2	3	0	254	188	84.67	1	1	2
Total	**16**	**27**	**3**	**1069**	**188**	**44.54**	**3**	**6**	**13**

In Irani Trophy (for Karnataka and Rest of India)

Season	*Mts*	*Inns*	*No*	*Runs*	*HSAvge*	*100s*	*50s*	*Cts*	
1993-94	1	2	0	122	93	61.00	0	1	1
1994-95	1	2	1	172	132*	172.00	1	0	2
Total	**2**	**4**	**1**	**294**	**132***	**98.00**	**1**	**1**	**3**

In Tests

Season	*Against*	*In*	*Mts*	*Inns*	*No*	*Runs*	*HS*	*Avge*	*100s*	*50s*	*Cts*
1996	ENG	ENG	2	3	0	187	95	62.33	0	2	1
1996-1997	AUS	IND	1	1	0	40	40	40.00	0	0	2
1996-1997	SA	IND	3	6	0	175	56	29.17	0	1	2
1996-1997	SA	SA	3	6	1	277	148	55.40	1	1	6
1996-1997	WI	WI	5	7	2	360	92	72.00	0	4	5
1997-1998	SL	SL	2	3	0	77	69	25.67	0	1	0
1997-1998	SL	IND	3	4	0	304	93	76.00	0	3	2
1997-1998	AUS	IND	3	5	0	223	86	44.60	0	3	6
1998-1999	ZIM	ZIM	1	2	0	162	118	81.00	1	0	2
1998-1999	NZ	NZ	2	4	1	321	190	107.00	2	0	4
1998-1999	PAK	IND	2	4	0	125	53	31.25	0	1	4
1998-1999	PAK	IND	1	2	0	37	24	18.50	0	0	1
1998-1999	SL	SL	1	1	0	107	107	107.00	1	0	0
1999-2000	NZ	IND	3	6	0	239	144	39.83	1	0	3
1999-2000	AUS	AUS	3	6	0	93	35	15.50	0	0	1

Season	*Against*	*In*	*Mts*	*Inns*	*No*	*Runs*	*HS*	*Avge*	*100s*	*50s*	*Cts*
2000-2001	BD	BD	1	2	1	69	41 *	69.00	0	0	1
2000-2001	ZIM	IND	2	3	2	432	200*	432.00	2	1	4
2000-2001	AUS	IND	3	6	0	338	180	56.33	1	1	6
2000-2001	ZIM	ZIM	2	3	1	138	68*	69.00	0	1	4
2001-2002	SL	SL	3	6	1	235	75	47.00	0	2	2
2001-2002	SA	SA	2	4	0	102	87	25.50	0	1	1
2001-2002	ENG	IND	3	4	1	122	86	40.67	0	1	3
2001-2002	ZIM	IND	2	3	0	72	65	24.00	0	1	7
2001-2002	WI	WI	5	8	1	404	144*	57.71	1	2	5
2002	ENG	ENG	4	6	0	602	217	100.33	3	1	10
2002-2003	WI	IND	3	5	2	148	100*	49.33	1	0	2
2002-2003	NZ	NZ	2	4	0	131	76	32.75	0	1	2
2003-2004	NZ	NZ	2	4	0	313	222	78.25	0	1	3
Home			**33**	**57**	**5**	**2662**	**222**	**51.19**	**6**	**13**	**46**
Away			**38**	**65**	**8**	**3265**	**217**	**57.28**	**9**	**16**	**44**
Total			**71**	**122**	**13**	**5927**	**222**	**54.37**	**15**	**29**	**90**

Against Each Country

Against	*Mts*	*Inns*	*No*	*Runs*	*HS*	*Avge*	*100s*	*50s*	*Cts*
Australia	10	18	0	694	180	38.55	1	4	15
Bangladesh	1	2	1	69	41*	69.00	0	0	1
England	9	13	1	911	217	75.91	3	4	14
New Zealand	9	18	1	1004	222	59.05	4	2	12
Pakistan	3	6	0	162	53	27.00	0	1	5
South Africa	10	20	1	648	148	34.10	1	3	10
Sri Lanka	9	14	1	723	107	55.61	1	6	4
West Indies	13	20	5	912	144*	60.80	2	6	12
Zimbabwe	7	11	3	804	200*	100.50	3	3	17
Total	**71**	**122**	**13**	**5927**	**222**	**53.47**	**15**	**29**	**90**

In Each Country

Against	*Mts*	*Inns*	*No*	*Runs*	*HS*	*Avge*	*100s*	*50s*	*Cts*
Australia	3	6	0	93	35	15.50	0	0	1
Bangladesh	1	2	1	69	41*	69.00	0	0	1
England	6	9	0	789	217	87.66	3	3	11
New Zealand	4	8	1	452	190	64.57	2	1	6
South Africa	5	10	1	379	148	42.11	1	2	7
Sri Lanka	6	10	1	419	107	46.55	1	3	2
West Indies	10	15	3	764	144*	63.66	1	6	10
Zimbabwe	3	5	1	300	118	75.00	1	1	6
	38	**65**	**8**	**3265**	**217**	**57.28**	**9**	**16**	**44**

Innings by Innings in Tests

No.	Date	Against	Venue	How Out	Runs	Result
1.	20 Jun, 1996	ENG	Lord's	ct. RC Russell b CC Lewis	95	Drawn
2.	4 July, 1996	ENG	Nottingham	ct. RC Russell b MA Ealham	84	Drawn
				ct. GP Thorpe b AD Mullally	8	
3.	10 Oct, 1996	AUS	New Delhi	ct. IA Healy b SR Waugh	40	Won by 7 wkts
4.	20 Nov, 1996	SA	Ahmedabad	lbw b PL Symocx	24	Won by 64 runs
				lbw b PL Symcox	34	
5.	27 Nov, 1996	SA	Kolkata	ct. AC Hudson b BM McMillan	31	Lost by 329 runs
				b BM McMillan	23	
6.	8 Dec, 1996	SA	Kanpur	lbw b PR Adams	7	Won by 280 runs
				ct. BM McMillan b PR Adams	56	
7.	26 Dec, 1996	SA	Durban	lbw b BM McMillan	7	Lost by 328 runs
				not out	27	
8.	2 Jan, 1997	SA	Cape Town	b L Klusener	2	Lost by 282 runs
				ct. DJ Richardson b PR Adams	12	
9.	16 Jan, 1997	SA	Johannesburg	ct. SM Pollock b WJ Cronje	148	Drawn
				ct. DJ Cullinan b PR Adams	81	
10.	6 Mar, 1997	WI	Kingston	ct. JR Murray b FA Rose	43	Drawn
				not out	51	
11.	14 Mar, 1997	WI	Port-of-Spain	bowled CEL Ambrose	57	Drawn

No.	Date	Against	Venue	How Out	Runs	Result
12.	27 Mar, 1997	WI	Bridgetown	bowled IR Bishop	78	Lost by 38 runs
				ct. CO Browne b FA Rose	2	
13.	4 Apr, 1997	WI	St. John's	not out	37	Drawn
14.	17 Apr, 1997	WI	Georgetown	ct. CL Hooper FA Rose	92	Drawn
15.	2 Aug, 1997	SL	Colombo (RPS)	c & b ST Jayasuriya	69	Drawn
16.	9 Aug, 1997	SL	Colombo (SSC)	ct. WPUJC Vaas b SC de Silva	2	Drawn
				ct. MS Atapattu b M Muralitharan	6	
17.	19 Nov, 1997	SL	Mohali	ct. A Ranatunga b ST Jayasuriya	34	Drawn
18.	26 Nov, 1997	SL	Nagpur	ct. MS Atapattu b WPUJC Vaas	92	Drawn
19.	3 Dec, 1997	SL	Mumbai	ct. RS Mahanama b HDPK Dharmasena	93	Drawn
				ct. PA de Silva b HDPK Dharmasena	85	
20.	6 Mar, 1998	AUS	Chennai	ct. GR Robertson b SK Warne	52	Won by 179 runs
				ct. IA Healy b SK Warne	56	
21.	18 Mar, 1998	AUS	Kolkata	c & b GS Blewett	86	Won by Inns & 219 runs
22.	25 Mar, 1998	AUS	Bangalore	bowled SK Warne	23	Lost by 8 wkts
				ct. IA Healy b GR Robertson	6	
23.	7 Oct, 1998	ZIM	Harare	ct. NC Johnson b M Mbangwa	118	Lost by 61 runs
				ct. A Flower b M Mbangwa	44	
24.	26 Dec, 1998	NZ	Wellington	lbw b SB Doull	0	Lost by 4 wkts
				bowled PJ Wiseman	28	

No.	*Date*	*Against*	*Venue*	*How Out*	*Runs*	*Result*
25.	2 Jan, 1999	NZ	Hamilton	ct. CD McMillan b CL Cairns	190	Drawn
				not out	103	
26.	28 Jan, 1999	PAK	Chennai	lbw b Saqlain Mushtaq	53	Lost by 12 runs
				bowled Wasim Akram	10	
27.	4 Feb, 1999	PAK	New Delhi	lbw b Saqlain Mushtaq	33	Won by 212 runs
				ct. Ijaz Ahmed b Saqlain Mushtaq	29	
28.	16 Feb, 1999	PAK	Kolkata	bowled Shoaib Akhtar	24	Lost by 46 runs
				ct. Moin Khan b Shoaib Akhtar	13	
29.	24 Feb, 1999	SL	Colombo (SSC)	ct. Ranatunga b UC Hathurusinghe	107	Drawn
30.	10 Oct, 1999	NZ	Mohali	ct. NJ Astle b CL Cairns	1	Drawn
				bowled DL Vettori	144	
31.	22 Oct, 1999	NZ	Kanpur	ct. AC Parore b DL Vettori	48	Won by 8 wkts
				lbw b DJ Nash	1	
32.	29 Oct, 1999	NZ	Ahmedabad	ct. AC Parore b DL Vettori	33	Drawn
				run out	12	
33.	10 Dec, 1999	AUS	Adelaide	ct. JL Langer b SK Warne	35	Lost by 285 runs
				ct. AC Gilchrist b SK Warne	6	
34.	26 Dec, 1999	AUS	Melbourne	ct. AC Gilchrist b B Lee	9	Lost by 180 runs
				ct. AC Gilchrist b B Lee	14	
35.	2 Jan, 2000	AUS	Sydney	ct. RT Ponting b GD McGrath	29	Lost by inns & 141 runs
				ct. SK Warne b GD McGrath	0	
36.	24 Feb, 2000	SA	Mumbai	bowled AA Donald	22	Lost by 4 wkts
				bowled SM Pollock	37	

No.	Date	Against	Venue	How Out	Runs	Result
37.	2 Mar, 2000	SA	Bangalore	ct. MV Boucher b WJ Cronje	17	Lost by inns & 71 runs
				ct. SM Pollock b N Boje	18	
38.	10 Nov, 2000	BD	Dhaka	ct. Al Sahariar b Mohd Rafique	28	Won by 9 wkts
				not out	41	
39.	18 Nov, 2000	ZIM	New Delhi	not out	200	Won by 7 wkts
				not out	70	
40.	25 Nov, 2000	ZIM	Nagpur	ct. A Flower b HH Streak	162	Drawn
41.	1 Mar, 2001	AUS	Mumbai	ct. AC Gilchrist b DW Fleming	9	Lost by 10 wkts
				bowled SK Warne	39	
42.	11 Mar, 2001	AUS	Kolkata	bowled SK Warne	25	Won by 171 runs
			run out	180		
43.	18 Mar, 2001	AUS	Chennai	ct. AC Gilchrist b JN Gillespie	81	Won by 2 wkts
				ct. SR Waugh b CR Miller	4	
44.	7 June, 2001	ZIM	Bulawayo	ct. A Flower b AM Blignaut	44	Won by 8 wkts
45.	15 June, 2001	ZIM	Harare	not out	68	Lost by 4 wkts
				ct. A Flower b AM Blignaut	26	
46.	14 Aug, 2001	SL	Galle	ct. RP Arnold b M Muralitharan	12	Lost by 10 wkts
				not out	61	
47.	22 Aug, 2001	SL	Kandy	lbw b WPUJC Vaas	15	Won by 7 wkts
				ct. RP Arnold b M Muralitharan	75	
48.	29 Aug, 2001	SL	Colombo (SSC)	ct. HP Thillakeratne b M Muralitharan	36	Lost by inns & 77 runs
				run out	36	

No.	Date	Against	Venue	How Out	Runs	Result
49.	3 Nov-2001	SA	Bloemfontein	ct. JH Kallis b SM Pollock	2	Lost by 9 wkts
				ct. G Kirsten b SM Pollock	11	
50.	16 Nov-2001	SA	Port Elizabeth	bowled SM Pollock	2	Drawn
				ct. MV Boucher b M Hayward	87	
51.	3 Dec, 2001	ENG	Mohali	lbw b J Ormond	86	Won by 10 wkts
52.	11 Dec, 2001	ENG	Ahmedabad	ct. JS Foster b MJ Hoggard	7	Drawn
				not out	26	
53.	19 Dec, 2001	ENG	Bangalore	ct. JS Foster b MJ Hoggard	3	Drawn
54.	21 Feb, 2002	ZIM	Nagpur	bowled HH Streak	65	Won by inns & 101 runs
55.	28 Feb, 2002	ZIM	New Delhi	run out	1	Won by 4 wkts
				ct. A Flower b RW Price	6	
56.	11 Apr, 2002	WI	Georgetown	not out	144	Drawn
57.	19 Apr, 2002	WI	Port-of-Spain	bowled MI Black	67	Won by 37 runs
				ct. JR Murray b CE Cuffy	36	
58.	2 May, 2002	WI	Bridgetown	run out	17	Lost by 10 wkts
				ct. RD Jacobs b A Sandford	14	
59.	10 May, 2002	WI	St. John's	bowled MW Dillon	91	Drawn
60.	18 May, 2002	WI	Kingston	lbw b MW Dillon	5	Lost by 155 runs
				lbw b A Sandford	30	
61.	25 July, 2002	ENG	Lord's	ct. MP Vaughan b MJ Hoggard	46	Lost by 170 runs
				bowled AF Giles	63	

No.	Date	Against	Venue	How Out	Runs	Result
62.	8 Aug, 2002	ENG	Nottingham	ct. RWT Key b MJ Hoggard	13	Drawn
				lbw b DG Cork	115	
63.	22 Aug, 2002	ENG	Leeds	st. AJ Stewart b AF Giles	148	Won by inns & 46 runs
64.	5 Sep, 2002	ENG	The Oval	run out	217	Drawn
65.	9 Oct, 2002	WI	Mumbai	retd. hurt	100	Won by Inns & 112 runs
66.	17 Oct, 2002	WI	Chennai	bowled JJC Lawson	11	Won by 8 wkts
				not out	6	
67.	30 Nov, 2002	WI	Kolkata	lbw b DB Powell	14	Drawn
				lbw b DB Powell	17	
68.	12 Dec, 2002	NZ	Wellington	bowled SB Styris	76	Lost by 10 wkts
				bowled SE Bond	7	
69.	19 Dec, 2002	NZ	Hamilton	ct. RG Hart b DR Tuffey	9	Lost by 4 wkts
				ct. sub b JDB Oram	39	
70.	8 Oct, 2003	NZ	Ahmedabad	ct. RG Hart b DL Vettori	222	Drawn
				ct. L Vincent b PJ Wiseman	73	
71.	16 Oct, 2003	NZ	Mchali	ct. RG Hart b I Butler	13	Drawn
				ct. SP Fleming b DR Tuffey	5	

Centuries

Runs	Balls	4s/6s	Against	Venue	Date
In Ranji Trophy (for Karnataka)					
215	346	26/2	Uttar Pradesh	Bangalore	19 Apr, 1998
210	392	27/2	Hyderabad	Bangalore	15 Nov, 1998
200*	291	23/0	Andhra Pradesh	Bangalore	27 Nov, 1992
191	285	20/0	Andhra Pradesh	Bangalore	10 Dec, 1994
153			Hyderabad	Bangalore	14 Mar, 1996
151*	320	15/0	Tamil Nadu	Bangalore	31 Dec, 1993
149	173	16/0	Rajasthan	Bangalore	16 Feb, 2000
138	260	18/2	Orissa	Rourkela	23 Feb, 1998
134	336	10/0	Bengal	Kolkata	16 Feb, 2001
128	227	16/0	Kerala	Bijapur	29 Jan, 1992
126			Goa	KGF	22 Nov, 1991
114	266	9/0	Tamil Nadu	Chennai	27 Mar, 1996
108	195	5/0	Goa	Bangalore	19 Dec, 1995
105*	220	7/0	Kerala	Bangalore	8 Jan, 1994

Runs	Balls	4s/6s	Against	Venue	Date
In Tests					
148			South Africa	Johannesburg	16 Jan, 1997
118	300	17/0	Zimbabwe	Harare	7 Oct, 1998
190	354	31/0	New Zealand	Hamilton	2 Jan, 1999
103*	136	16/0	New Zealand	Hamilton	2 Jan, 1999
107	218	12/0	Sri Lanka	Colombo (SSC)	24 Feb, 1999
144	327	18/0	New Zealand	Mohali	10 Oct, 1999
200*	350	20/0	Zimbabwe	New Delhi	18 Nov, 2000
162	301	20/0	Zimbabwe	Nagpur	25 Nov, 2000
180	353	21/0	Australia	Kolkata	11 Mar, 2001
144*	349	23/0	West Indies	Georgetown	11 Apr, 2002
115	244	16/0	England	Nottingham	8 Aug, 2002
148	307	23/0	England	Leeds	22 Aug, 2002
217	468	28/3	England	The Oval	5 Sep, 2002
100	242	12/0	West Indies	Mumbai	9 Oct, 2002
222	387	28/1	New Zealand	Ahmedabad	8 Oct, 2003

Runs	Balls	4s/6s	Against	Venue	Date
In Duleep Trophy (for South Zone)					
188			West Zone	Surat	18 Jan, 2001
148	258	12/1	East Zone	Jamshedpur	25 Oct, 1994
101*	251	10/0	West Zone	Alwar	10 Nov, 1995
In Irani Trophy (for Rest of India)					
132*	206	11/1	Mumbai	Mumbai	12 Oct, 1994
For Kent during 2000 Season					
137			Hampshire	Portsmouth	19 July, 2000
In Other First-class Matches					
145*	270	23/0	BP XI v. NZL	Rajkot	7 Oct, 1995
137			Ind v. Zim A	Mutare	28 May, 2001
107	257	5/0	Ind v. Tasmania	Hobart	17 Dec, 1999
101*			Ind v. Brit Univ	Cambridge	26 June, 1996

Century Partnerships

No.	Wkt	Runs	Partner	Against	Venue	Season
In Ranji Trophy (for Karnataka)						
1.	3rd	262	Vijay Bharadwaj	Tamil Nadu	Chennai	1995-96
2.	3rd	163	Saldanha, C	Kerala	Bijapur	1991-92
3.	3rd	154	Srinath, K	Madhya Pradesh	Bangalore	1992-93
4.	3rd	148	Vijay Bharadwaj	Hyderabad	Secunderabad	1997-98
5.	3rd	115*	Shashikanth, PV	Andhra Pradesh	Bangalore	1992-93
6.	3rd	115	Thilak Naidu, VS	Rajasthan	Bangalore	1999-2000
7.	3rd	110	Srinath, K	Hyderabad	Hubli	1992-93
8.	4th	257	Vijay Bharadwaj	Uttar Pradesh	Bangalore	1997-98
9.	4th	241	Jeshwanth, K	Andhra Pradesh	Bangalore	1994-95
10.	4th	120	Kirmani, SMH	Kerala	Bijapur	1991-92
11.	4th	108	Vijay Bharadwaj	Orissa	Rourkela	1997-98
12.	4th	101	Vijay Bharadwaj	Punjab	Bangalore	1997-98
13.	5th	299	Arjun Raja, VK	Bengal	Kolkata	1990-91
14.	5th	153	Kirmani, SMH	Andhra Pradesh	Bangalore	1992-93
15.	5th	102	Arun Kumar, J	Hyderabad	Secunderabad	1997-98
16.	6th	238	Jeshwanth, K	Maharashtra	Pune	1990-91

No.	Wkt	Runs	Partner	Against	Venue	Season
17.	6th	142	Vaidya, A	Andhra Pradesh	Bangalore	1992-93
18.	7th	262	Shiruguppi, S	Hyderabad	Bangalore	1998-99
In Tests						
1.	2nd	232	Ramesh, S	Sri Lanka	Colombo (SSC)	1998-99
2.	2nd	171	Dasguptha, D	South Africa	Port Elizabeth	2001-2002
3.	2nd	170	Bangar, SB	England	Leeds	2002
4.	2nd	155	Shivsundar Das	Zimbabwe	Nagpur	2000-2001
5.	2nd	155	Wasim Jaffer	West Indies	St. John's	2001-2002
6.	2nd	147	Sidhu, NS	Sri Lanka	Colombo (SSC)	1997-98
7.	2nd	137	Sidhu, NS	Sri Lanka	Nagpur	1997-98
8.	2nd	137	Sidhu, NS	Sri Lanka	Nagpur	1997-98
9.	2nd	130	Shivsundar Das	Zimbabwe	Nagpur	2001-2002
10.	2nd	126	Sehwag, V	England	Lord's	2002
11.	2nd	107	Shivsundar Das	Zimbabwe	New Delhi	2000-2001
12.	3rd	249	Tendulkar, SR	Zimbabwe	Nagpur	2000-2001
13.	3rd	229	Tendulkar, SR	New Zealand	Mohali	1999-2000
14.	3rd	229	Tendulkar, SR	New Zealand	Mohali	1999-2000
15.	3rd	213	Tendulkar, SR	Zimbabwe	New Delhi	2000-2001
16.	3rd	194*	Ganguly, SC	New Zealand	Hamilton	1998-99

No.	*Wkt*	*Runs*	*Partner*	*Against*	*Venue*	*Season*
17.	3rd	163	Tendulkar, SR	England	Nottingham	2002
18.	3rd	160	Ganguly, SC	Sri Lanka	Mumbai	1997-98
19.	3rd	160	Ganguly, SC	Sri Lanka	Mumbai	1997-98
20.	3rd	150	Tendulkar, SR	England	Leeds	2002
21.	3rd	140	Tendulkar, SR	Australia	Kolkata	1997-98
22.	3rd	136	Dasguptha, D	England	Mohali	2001-2002
23.	3rd	124	Tendulkar, SR	West Indies	Port of Spain	2001-2002
24.	3rd	113	Tendulkar, SR	Australia	Chennai	1997-98
25.	3rd	109	Tendulkar, SR	New Zealand	Hamilton	1998-99
26.	4th	135	Ganguly, SC	England	Nottingham	2002
27.	4th	105	Ganguly, SC	England	The Oval	2002
28.	5th	376	Laxman, VVS	Australia	Kolkata	2000-2001
29.	5th	169	Tendulkar, SR	Australia	Chennai	2000-2001
30.	5th	119	Laxman, VVS	West Indies	Georgetown	2001-2002
31.	5th	113	Laxman, VVS	England	The Oval	2002
32.	5th	105	Laxman, VVS	West Indies	Mumbai	2002-2003
33.	6th	165	Azharuddin, M	South Africa	Kanpur	1996-97
34.	8th	144	Srinath, J	New Zealand	Hamilton	1998-99
35.	8th	120*	Sarandeep Singh	West Indies	Georgetown	2001-2002

No.	Wkt	Runs	Partner	Against	Venue	Season
In Duleep Trophy (for South Zone)						
1.	3rd	409	Laxman, VVS	West Zone	Surat	2000-2001
2.	3rd	199	Laxman, VVS	West Zone	Alwar	1995-96
3.	3rd	144	Raman, WV	North Zone	Nagpur	1995-96
4.	3rd	136	Laxman, VVS	East Zone	Lucknow	1995-96
5.	3rd	123	Raman, WV	West Zone	Rourkela	1994-95
6.	3rd	113	Arun Kumar, J	East Zone	Jamshedpur	1994-95
7.	3rd	108	Raman, WV	East Zone	Jamshedpur	1994-95
8.	4th	126	Robin Singh	East Zone	Jamshedpur	1994-95
In Irani Trophy (for Rest of India)						
1.	6th	224	Yadav, V	Mumbai	Mumbai	1994-95
2.	6th	145	Jedhe, SV	Punjab	Ludhiana	1993-94
In Other First Class Matches						
1.	2nd	178	Laxman, VVS	Jamaica	Kingston	1996-97
2.	2nd	175	Gambhir, G	ZIM	Vijayawada	2001-2002
3.	2nd	160	Mongia, NR	BU	Cambridge	1996
4.	3rd	173	Azharuddin, M	NZL	Rourkela	1995-96

No.	Wkt	Runs	Partner	Against	Venue	Season
5.	3rd	136*	Ganguly, SC	Wellington	Wellington	1998-99
6.	3rd	119	Rathore, V	ENG A	Kolkata	1994-95
7.	4th	153*	Azharuddin, M	Leicestershire	Leicester	1996
8.	4th	118	Rizwan Shamshad	ENG XI	Chennai	1994-95
9.	4th	104	Wells, AP	Zimbabwe	Canterbury	2000
10.	5th	208	Hockley	Zimbabwe	Canterbury	2000
11.	5th	121	Robin Singh	NZL	Rajkot	1995-96
12.	6th	227	Dighe, SS	ZIM A	Mutare	2001-2002
13.	6th	124	Tendulkar, SR	Worcestershire	Worcester	2002
For Kent in English County in the Year 2000						
1.	2nd	140	Key, RWT	Derbyshire	Derby	2000
2.	2nd	129	Key, RWT	Somerset	Maidstone	2000
3.	2nd	115	Key, RWT	Hampshire	Portsmouth	2000
4.	3rd	130	Wells, AP	Somerset	Maidstone	2000

In One-day Internationals

Season by Season

Season	*In*	*Vs*	*Mts*	*Inns*	*Nos*	*Runs*	*HS*	*Avge*	*100s*	*50s*	*cts/sts*
1995-96	SIN	Singer	2	2	0	7	4	3.50	0	0	3
1995-96	UAE	Pepsi	2	2	0	14	11	7.00	0	0	2
1996	ENG	ENG	1	1	1	22	22*		0	0	2
1996-97	SL	Singer	3	2	1	20	13	20.00	0	0	1
1996-97	CAN	PAK	5	5	0	220	90	44.00	0	1	4
1996-97	IND	Titan	6	6	0	176	62	29.33	0	2	2
1996-97	IND	SA	1	1	0	16	16	16.00	0	0	0
1996-97	SA	SA	8	8	0	280	84	35.00	0	3	3
1996-97	WI	WI	4	3	0	121	74	40.33	0	1	1
1996-97	IND	Independence	3	3	1	189	107	94.50	1	1	0
1997-98	SL	Asia	4	2	0	76	69	38.00	0	1	2
1997-98	SL	SL	4	4	0	139	78	34.75	0	1	2
1997-98	CAN	PAK	6	4	1	65	25	21.67	0	0	1
1997-98	PAK	PAK	1	1	0	50	50	50.00	0	1	0
1997-98	UAE	Akai	1	1	0	31	31	31.00	0	0	0

Season	*In*	*Vs*	*Mts*	*Inns*	*Nos*	*Runs*	*HS*	*Avge*	*100s*	*50s*	*cts/sts*
1997-98	IND	Cola	4	4	0	88	49	22.00	0	0	4
1998-99	CAN	PAK	4	4	0	32	18	8.00	0	0	2
1998-99	ZIM	ZIM	3	2	0	92	64	46.00	0	1	0
1998-99	BD	Mini WC	2	2	0	68	48	34.00	0	0	2
1998-99	UAE	Cola	1	1	0	3	3	3.00	0	0	1
1998-99	NZ	NZ	5	5	1	309	123*	77.25	1	2	1
1998-99	IND	Pepsi	5	5	0	161	116	32.20	1	0	1
1998-99	UAE	Cola	5	5	0	188	81	37.60	0	2	2/1
1999	ENG	WC	8	8	1	461	145	65.86	2	3	2
1999-2000	SL	Aiwa	4	4	0	40	22	10.00	0	0	4
1999-2000	SIN	Cola	4	4	1	183	103*	61.00	1	0	3/0
1999-2000	CAN	WI	3	3	0	98	77	32.67	0	1	4
1999-2000	KEN	LG	4	4	1	81	30	27.00	0	0	5
1999-2000	IND	NZ	5	5	1	240	153	60.00	1	0	4
1999-2000	AUS	CUS	8	8	0	268	65	33.50	0	3	7
1999-2000	IND	SA	5	5	0	208	79	41.60	0	2	2
1999-2000	UAE	Cola	4	4	0	89	29	22.25	0	0	0
1999-2000	BD	Asia	3	2	0	50	26	25.00	0	0	3

Season	*In*	*Vs*	*Mts*	*Inns*	*Nos*	*Runs*	*HS*	*Avge*	*100s*	*50s*	*cts/sts*
2000-2001	KEN	ICC	4	4	1	157	68*	52.33	0	2	1
2000-2001	UAE	Cola	2	2	0	101	85	50.50	0	1	0
2000-2001	IND	ZIM	5	4	0	107	62	26.75	0	1	2
2000-2001	IND	AUS	5	5	0	146	80	29.20	0	1	1
2001-2002	ZIM	Cola	5	4	1	121	72*	40.33	0	1	2
2001-2002	SL	Cola	7	7	2	259	57*	51.80	0	1	3
2001-2002	SA	SBT	7	5	1	214	77	53.50	0	3	2/3
2001-2002	IND	ZIM	5	5	1	153	66*	38.25	0	1	3
2001-2002	WI	WI	3	3	1	57	28	28.50	0	0	1/1
2002	ENG	Natwest	6	6	1	245	82	49.00	0	3	6/3
2002-2003	SL	ICC	5	2	0	120	71	60.00	0	1	5
2002-2003	IND	WI	7	6	2	300	109*	75.00	1	2	6/1
2002-2003	NZ	NZ	7	7	0	116	21	16.57	0	0	8
2002-2003	SA	WC	11	10	5	318	62	63.60	0	2	15/1
			207	**190**	**24**	**6499**	**153**	**39.15**	**8**	**44**	**125/10**

Against Each Country

Against	*Mts*	*Inns*	*Nos*	*Runs*	*HS*	*Avge*	*100s*	*50s*	*cts/sts*
Australia	19	19	0	543	80	28.58	0	5	12/1
Bangladesh	4	2	0	6	5	3.00	0	0	2/0
England	9	8	2	376	82	62.67	0	5	10/2
Kenya	10	8	3	328	104*	65.60	1	1	5/2
Namibia	1	0	0	0	0		0	0	2/0
Holland	1	1	0	17	17	17.00	0	0	3/0
New Zealand	24	24	5	889	153	46.79	2	4	18/0
Pakistan	35	32	2	862	107	28.73	1	4	16/0
South Africa	27	27	2	1014	84	40.56	0	11	14/1
Sri Lanka	26	24	3	902	145	42.95	2	4	15/2
West Indies	25	23	4	847	109*	44.58	2	4	14/2
Zimbabwe	26	22	3	715	85	37.63	0	6	14/0
	207	**190**	**24**	**6499**	**153**	**39.15**	**8**	**44**	**125/10**

Year-wise Performance (Test)

Year	*Mts*	*Inns*	*No*	*Runs*	*HS*	*Avge*	*100s*	*50s*	*Cts*
1996	7	12	1	436	95	39.64	0	3	6
1996	20	19	2	475	90	27.94	0	3	14/0
1997	31	26	2	951	107	39.63	1	8	9/0
1998	14	13	0	283	64	21.77	0	1	9/0
1999	43	43	5	1761	153	46.34	6	8	26/1
2000	31	29	1	980	85	35.00	0	9	15/0
2001	24	21	4	740	80	43.53	0	6	8/3
2002	28	24	5	913	108 *	48.05	1	7	25/5
2003	16	15	5	396	62	39.60	0	2	19/1
	207	**190**	**24**	**6499**	**153**	**39.15**	**8**	**44**	**125/10**

Innings by Innings

No.	Against	In	Date	Venue	How Out	Fielder	Bowler	Runs	Cts/Sts
1.	SL	SING	3 Apr, 1996	Singapore	caught	Kaluwitharana, RS	Muralitharan, M	3	2
2.	PAK	SING	5 Apr, 1996	Singapore	run out			4	1
3.	PAK	SING	12 Apr, 1996	Singapore	caught	Rashid Latif	Mushtaq Ahmed	3	0
4.	SA	UAE	14 Apr, 1996	Sharjah	caught	Rhodes, JN	Pollock, SM	11	2
5.	ENG	ENG	26 May, 1996	Manchester	not out			22	2
6.	SL	SL	28 Aug, 1996	Colombo (RPS)	not out			7	0
7.	ZIM	SL	1 Sept, 1996	Colombo (SSC)	dnb				1/1
8.	AUS	SL	6 Sept, 1996	Colombo (SSC)	bowled		Reiffel, PR	13	1
9.	PAK	CAN	16 Sept, 1996	Toronto	caught	Aamir Sohail	Salim Malk	39	1
10.	PAK	CAN	17 Sept, 1996	Toronto	bowled		Saqlain Mushtaq	90	1
11.	PAK	CAN	18 Sept, 1996	Toronto	caught	Salim Elahi	Saqlain Mushtaq	46	0
12.	PAK	CAN	21 Sept, 1996	Toronto	caught	Moin Khan	Saqlain Mushtaq	25	0
13.	PAK	CAN	23 Sept, 1996	Toronto	caught	Shahid Nazir	Mushtaq Ahmed	20	2
14.	SA	IND	17 Oct, 1996	Hyderabad	caught	Rhodes, JN	Crookes, D	62	0
15.	AUS	IND	21 Oct, 1996	Bangalore	lbw		Fleming, DW	6	0
16.	SA	IND	23 Oct, 1996	Jaipur	caught	Richardson, RB	McMillan, BM	0	0
17.	SA	IND	29 Oct, 1996	Rajkot	run out			21	0

No.	Against	In	Date	Venue	How Out	Fielder	Bowler	Runs	Cts/Sts
18.	AUS	IND	3 Nov, 1996	Mohali	caught	Taylor, MA	Law, SG	56	0
19.	SA	IND	6 Nov, 1996	Mumbai	bowled		De Villiers, PS	31	2
20.	SA	IND	14 Dec, 1996	Mumbai	run out			16	0
21.	SA	SA	23 Jan, 1997	Bloemfontein	bowled		Symcox, PL	8	0
22.	ZIM	SA	27 Jan, 1997	Paarl	run out			23	0
23.	SA	SA	2 Feb, 1997	Port Elizabeth	caught	Cronje, WJ	Donald, AA	50	0
24.	SA	SA	4 Feb, 1997	East London	run out			53	1
25.	ZIM	SA	7 Feb, 1997	Centurion	caught	Flower, A	Rennie, J	12	0
26.	ZIM	SA	10 Feb, 1997	Benoni	bowled		Whittal, GJ	17	1
27.	SA	SA	12 Feb, 1997	Durban	caught	Kirsten, G	Cronje, WJ	33	0
28.	SA	SA	13 Feb, 1997	Durban	caught	Kirsten, G	Klusener, L	84	1
29.	WI	WI	26 Apr, 1997	Port-of-Spain	caught	Hooper, CL	Rose, FA	17	0
30.	WI	WI	27 Apr, 1997	Port-of-Spain	dnb				0
31.	WI	WI	30 Apr, 1997	Kingstown	bowled		Gibson, OD	74	1
32.	WI	WI	3 May, 1997	Bridgetown	caught	Chanderpaul, S	Rose, FA	30	0
33.	NZ	IND	14 May, 1997	Bangalore	not out			21	0
34.	SL	IND	17 May, 1997	Mumbai	bowled		Muralitharan, M	61	0
35.	PAK	IND	21 May, 1997	Chennai	caught	Shahid Afridi	Aaqib Javed	107	0
36.	SL	SL	18 July, 1997	Colombo (RPS)	bowled		Jayasuriya, ST	69	1

No.	Against	In	Date	Venue	How Out	Fielder	Bowler	Runs	Cts/Sts
37.	PAK	SL	20 Jul, 1997	Colombo (SSC)	dnb				
38.	BD	SL	24 Jul, 1997	Colombo (SSC)	dnb				0
39.	SL	SL	26 Jul, 1997	Colombo (RPS)	caught	Mahanama, RS	Vaas, WPUJC	7	0
40.	SL	SL	17 Aug, 1997	Colombo (RPS)	run out			1	0
41.	SL	SL	20 Aug, 1997	Colombo (RPS)	caught	de Silva, SKL	Jayasuriya, ST	18	0
42.	SL	SL	23 Aug, 1997	Colombo (SSC)	caught	Kalpage, RS	de Silva, PA	78	2
43.	SL	SL	24 Aug, 1997	Colombo (SSC)	caught	Chandana, U	Jayasuriya, ST	42	0
44.	PAK	CAN	13 Sep, 1997	Toronto	caught	Ijaz Ahmed	Shahid Afridi	23	0
45.	PAK	CAN	14 Sep, 1997	Toronto	run out			14	0
46.	PAK	CAN	17 Sep, 1997	Toronto	dnb				0
47.	PAK	CAN	18 Sep, 1997	Toronto	caught	Saaed Anwar	Salim Malik	25	1
48.	PAK	CAN	20 Sep, 1997	Toronto	dnb				0
49.	PAK	CAN	21 Sep, 1997	Toronto	not out			3	0
50.	PAK	PAK	28 Sep, 1997	Hyderabad (P)	bowled		Aaqib Javed	50	0
51.	WI	UAE	16 Dec, 1997	Sharjah	bowled		Hooper, CL	31	0
52.	BD	IND	14 May, 1998	Mohali	c & b		Athar Ali Khan	5	1
53.	KEN	IND	20 May, 1998	Bangalore	bowled		Aasif Karim	49	1
54.	BD	IND	25 May, 1998	Mumbai	bowled		Mohd Rafique	1	1
55.	KEN	IND	28 May, 1998	Gwalior	caught	Vadher, A	Tikolo, SO	33	1

No.	*Against*	*In*	*Date*	*Venue*	*How Out*	*Fielder*	*Bowler*	*Runs*	*Cts/Sts*
56.	PAK	CAN	12 Sep, 1998	Toronto	caught	Moin Khan	Abdur Razzak	4	0
57.	PAK	CAN	13 Sep, 1998	Toronto	c & b		Abdur Razzak	18	1
58.	PAK	CAN	16 Sep, 1998	Toronto	bowled		Mohd Zahid	9	0
59.	PAK	CAN	19 Sep, 1998	Toronto	run out			1	1
60.	ZIM	ZIM	26 Sep, 1998	Bulawayo	caught	Campbell, ADR	Brent, GB	64	0
61.	ZIM	ZIM	27 Sep, 1998	Bulawayo	dnb				
62.	ZIM	ZIM	30 Sep, 1998	Harare	caught	Streak, HH	Whittall, AR	28	0
63.	AUS	BD	28 Oct, 1998	Dhaka	run out			48	2
64.	WI	BD	31 Oct, 1998	Dhaka	caught	Williams, SC	Hooper, CL	20	0
65.	ZIM	UAE	11 Nov, 1998	Sharjah	caught	Goodwin, MW	Olonga, HK	3	1
66.	NZ	NZ	9 Jan, 1999	Taupo	not out			123	0
67.	NZ	NZ	12 Jan, 1999	Napier	caught	Parore, AC	Vettori, DL	38	0
68.	NZ	NZ	14 Jan, 1999	Wellington	caught	Twose, RG	Larsen, GR	68	1
69.	NZ	NZ	16 Jan, 1999	Auckland	bowled		Cairns, CL	51	0
70.	NZ	NZ	19 Jan, 1999	Christchurch	caught	Harris, CZ	Vettori, DL	29	0
71.	SL	IND	22 Mar, 1999	Nagpur	caught	Boteju, H	Vaas, WPUJC	116	0
72.	PAK	IND	24 Mar, 1999	Jaipur	bowled		Shoaib Akhtar	3	0
73.	SL	IND	30 Mar, 1999	Pune	caught	Ranatunga, A	Upashantha, KEA	17	0
74.	PAK	IND	1 Apr, 1999	Mohali	caught	Shahid Afridi	Shoaib Akhtar	0	1

No.	Against	In	Date	Venue	How Out	Fielder	Bowler	Runs	Cts/Sts
75.	PAK	IND	4 Apr, 1999	Bangalore	lbw		Azhar Mahmood	25	0
76.	PAK	UAE	8 Apr, 1999	Sharjah	caught	Ijaz Ahmed	Shahid Afridi	28	0
77.	ENG	UAE	9 Apr, 1999	Sharjah	c & b		Hick, GA	16	1/1
78.	ENG	UAE	11 Apr, 1999	Sharjah	run out			63	0
79.	PAK	UAE	13 Apr, 1999	Sharjah	run out			81	1
80.	PAK	UAE	16 Apr, 1999	Sharjah	lbw		Wasim Akram	0	0
81.	SA	ENG	15 May, 1999	Brighton	bowled		Klusener, L	54	0
82.	ZIM	ENG	19 May, 1999	Leicester	caught	Flower, GW	Streak, HH	13	0
83.	KEN	ENG	23 May, 1999	Bristol	not out			104	0
84.	SL	ENG	26 May, 1999	Taunton	run out			145	0/0
85.	ENG	ENG	29 May, 1999	Birmingham	caught	Ealham, MA	Flintoff, A	53	0
86.	AUS	ENG	4 June, 1999	The Oval	caught	Gilchrist, AC	McGrath, GD	2	0
87.	PAK	ENG	8 Jun, 1999	Manchester	caught	Shahid Afridi	Wasim Akram	61	0
88.	NZ	ENG	12 Jun, 1999	Nottingham	caught	Fleming, SP	Cairns, CL	29	2
89.	AUS	SL	23 Aug, 1999	Galle	caught	Gilchrist, AC	Symonds, A	5	1
90.	SL	SL	25 Aug, 1999	Colombo (RPS)	caught	Kaluwitharana, RS	Vaas, WPUJC	22	0
91.	AUS	SL	28 Aug, 1999	Colombo (SSC)	caught	Gilchrist, AC	Gillespie, JN	0	2/0
92.	SL	SL	29 Aug, 1999	Colombo (SSC)	caught	Kaluwitharana, RS	Chandana, UDU	13	1/0
93.	ZIM	SING	4 Sep, 1999	Singapore	caught	Johnson, NC	Blignaut, AM	12	2/0

No.	Against	In	Date	Venue	How Out	Fielder	Bowler	Runs	Cts/Sts
94.	WI	SING	5 Sep, 1999	Singapore	caught	Bryan, HR	McLean, NAM	39	0
95.	WI	SING	7 Sep, 1999	Singapore	caught	Campbell, SL	King, RD	29	0/0
96.	WI	SING	8 Sep, 1999	Singapore	not out			103	1/0
97.	WI	CAN	11 Sep, 1999	Toronto	caught	Jacobs, RD	Walsh, CA	5	0
98.	WI	CAN	12 Sep, 1999	Toronto	lbw		Dillon, M	16	0
99.	WI	CAN	14 Sep, 1999	Toronto	bowled		Dillon, M	77	4
100.	SA	KEN	26 Sep, 1999	Nairobi	not out			9	2
101.	KEN	KEN	29 Sep, 1999	Nairobi	caught	Vadher, AV	Odumbe, MO	30	0
102.	ZIM	KEN	1 Oct, 1999	Nairobi	lbw		Goodwin, MW	12	2
103.	SA	KEN	3 Oct, 1999	Nairobi	caught	Rhodes, JN	Crookes, DN	30	1
104.	NZ	IND	5 Nov, 1999	Rajkot	lbw		Astle, NJ	39	2
105.	NZ	IND	8 Nov, 1999	Hyderabad	caught	Fleming, SP	Cairns, CL	153	0
106.	NZ	IND	11 Nov, 1999	Gwalior	caught	Horne, MJ	Tait, AR	14	1
107.	NZ	IND	14 Nov, 1999	Guwahati	caught	Parore, AC	Cairns, CL	5	0
108.	NZ	IND	17 Nov, 1999	New Delhi	not out			29	1
109.	PAK	AUS	10 Jan, 2000	Brisbane	caught	Moin Khan	Shoaib Akhtar	8	1
110.	AUS	AUS	12 Jan, 2000	Melbourne	caught	Martyn, DR	Lee, S	60	0
111.	AUS	AUS	14 Jan, 2000	Sydney	lbw		Symonds, A	22	1
112.	PAK	AUS	21 Jan, 2000	Hobart	lbw		Wasim Akram	15	0

No.	Against	In	Date	Venue	How Out	Fielder	Bowler	Runs	Cts/Sts
113.	PAK	AUS	25 Jan, 2000	Adelaide	caught	Inzamam-ul-Haq	Shahid Afridi	32	1
114.	AUS	AUS	26 Jan, 2000	Adelaide	caught	Gilchrist, AC	Lee, S	63	3
115.	PAK	AUS	28 Jan, 2000	Perth	caught	Moin Khan	Wasim Akram	3	1
116.	AUS	AUS	30 Jan, 2000	Perth	caught	Waugh, ME	Lee, S	65	0
117.	SA	IND	9 Mar, 2000	Kochi	caught	Williams, HS	Cronje, WJ	17	0
118.	SA	IND	12 Mar, 2000	Jamshedpur	caught	Gibbs, HH	Boje, N	36	0
119.	SA	IND	15 Mar, 2000	Faridabad	run out			73	0
120.	SA	IND	17 Mar, 2000	Baroda	caught	Cronje, WJ	Boje, N	3	0
121.	SA	IND	19 Mar, 2000	Nagpur	run out			79	1
122.	SA	UAE	22 Mar, 2000	Sharjah	bowled		Kallis, JH	8	0
123.	PAK	UAE	23 Mar, 2000	Sharjah	caught	Shoaib Malik	Abdur Razzaq	26	0
124.	PAK	UAE	26 Mar, 2000	Sharjah	caught	Moin Khan	Shoaib Akhtar	29	0
125.	SA	UAE	27 Mar, 2000	Sharjah	caught	McKenzie, ND	Klusener, L	26	0
126.	BD	BD	30 May, 2000	Dhaka	dnb				0
127.	SL	BD	1 June, 2000	Dhaka	c & b		Muralitharan, M	24	2/0
128.	PAK	BD	3 June, 2000	Dhaka	lbw		Abdur Razzaq	26	1
129.	KEN	KEN	3 Oct, 2000	Nairobi	not out			68	1
130.	AUS	KEN	7 Oct, 2000	Nairobi	caught	Lee, S	Gillespie, JN	9	0
131.	SA	KEN	13 Oct, 2000	Nairobi	caught	Boucher, MV	Klusener, L	58	0

No.	Against	In	Date	Venue	How Out	Fielder	Bowler	Runs	Cts/Sts
132.	NZ	KEN	15 Oct, 2000	Nairobi	run out			22	0
133.	SL	UAE	20 Oct, 2000	Sharjah	run out			16	0
134.	ZIM	UAE	22 Oct, 2000	Sharjah	caught	Flower, GW	Viljoen, DP	85	0
135.	ZIM	IND	2 Dec, 2000	Cuttack	run out			9	0
136.	ZIM	IND	5 Dec, 2000	Ahmedabad	run out			62	1
137.	ZIM	IND	8 Dec, 2000	Jodhpur	caught	Rennie, GJ	Flower, GW	30	0
138.	ZIM	IND	11 Dec, 2000	Kanpur	dnb				0
139.	ZIM	IND	14 Dec, 2000	Rajkot	caught	Streak, HH	Strang, BC	6	1
140.	AUS	IND	25 Mar, 2001	Bangalore	caught	Harvey, IJ	Martyn, DR	80	1
141.	AUS	IND	28 Mar, 2001	Pune	run out			13	0
142.	AUS	IND	31 Mar, 2001	Indore	caught	Gilchrist, AC	Fleming, DW	15	0
143.	AUS	IND	3 Apr, 2001	Vishakapatnam	c & b		Warne, SK	7	0
144.	AUS	IND	6 Apr, 2001	Margao	caught	Waugh, SR	Symonds, A	31	0
145.	ZIM	ZIM	24 June, 2001	Harare	dnb				1
146.	ZIM	ZIM	27 June, 2001	Bulwayo	not out			72	0
147.	WI	ZIM	30 June, 2001	Bulwayo	stumped	Jacobs, RD	Nagamootoo, MV	4	0
148.	WI	ZIM	4 July, 2001	Harare	bowled		Gayle, CH	15	1
149.	WI	ZIM	7 July, 2001	Harare	bowled		King, RD	30	0

No.	Against	In	Date	Venue	How Out	Fielder	Bowler	Runs	Cts/Sts
150.	NZ	SL	20 Jul, 2001	Colombo (RPS)	caught	Sinclair, MS	Nash, DJ	15	0
151.	SL	SL	22 Jul, 2001	Colombo (RPS)	not out			49	0
152.	NZ	SL	26 Jul, 2001	Colombo (RPS)	bowled		Oram, JDP	27	2
153.	SL	SL	28 Jul, 2001	Colombo (RPS)	caught	Kaluwitharana, RS	Vaas, WPUJC	43	0
154.	SL	SL	1 Aug, 2001	Colombo (SSC)	stumped	Kaluwitharana, RS	Jayasuriya, ST	47	1
155.	NZ	SL	2 Aug, 2001	Colombo (SSC)	not out			57	0
156.	SL	SL	5 Aug, 2001	Colombo (RPS)	bowled		Fernando, CRD	21	0
157.	SA	SA	5 Oct, 2001	Johannesburg	caught	McKenzie, ND	Nel, A	1	1
158.	SA	SA	10 Oct, 2001	Centurion	caught	Klusener, L	Pollock, SM	54	1
159.	KEN	SA	12 Oct, 2001	Bloemfontein	dnb				0
160.	KEN	SA	17 Oct, 2001	Port Elizabeth	caught	Otieno, DO	Suji, AO	11	0
161.	SA	SA	19 Oct, 2001	East London	not out			71	0
162.	KEN	SA	24 Oct, 2001	Paarl	dnb				0/2
163.	SA	SA	26 Oct, 2001	Durban	caught	Pollock, SM	Kemp, JM	77	0/1
164.	ZIM	IND	7 Mar, 2002	Faridabad	lbw		Flower, GW	23	0
165.	ZIM	IND	10 Mar, 2002	Mohali	not out			66	0
166.	ZIM	IND	13 Mar, 2002	Kochi	caught	Wishart, CB	Mbangwa, M	6	
167.	ZIM	IND	16 Mar, 2002	Hyderabad	bowled		Flower, GW	32	2
168.	ZIM	IND	19 Mar, 2002	Guwahati	bowled		Hondo, DT	26	1

No.	Against	In	Date	Venue	How Out	Fielder	Bowler	Runs	Cts/Sts
169.	WI	WI	29 May, 2002	Bridgetown	not out			9	1/1
170.	WI	WI	1 Jun, 2002	Port-of-Spain	bowled		Hooper, CL	28	0/0
171.	WI	WI	2 Jun, 2002	Port-of-Spain	caught	Sarwan, RR	Hooper, CL	20	0/0
172.	ENG	ENG	29 Jun, 2002	Lord's	not out			73	2/1
173.	SL	ENG	30 Jun, 2002	The Oval	bowled		Chandana, UDU	8	3/0
174.	ENG	ENG	4 Jul, 2002	Chester-le-Street	caught	Flintoff, A	Collingwood, PD	82	0/0
175.	SL	ENG	6 Jul, 2002	Birmingham	run out			64	1/0
176.	SL	ENG	11 Jul, 2002	Bristol	lbw		Chandana, UDU	13	0/2
177.	ENG	ENG	13 Jul, 2002	Lord's	caught	Knight, NV	Irani, RC	5	0/0
178.	ZIM	SL	14 Sep, 2002	Colombo (RPS)	run out			71	1/0
179.	ENG	SL	22 Sep, 2002	Colombo (RPS)	dnb				2/0
180.	SA	SL	25 Sep, 2002	Colombo (RPS)	lbw		Klusener, L	49	1/0
181.	SL	SL	28 Sep, 2002	Colombo (RPS)	dnb				1/0
182.	SL	SL	30 Sep, 2002	Colombo (RPS)	dnb				0
183.	WI	IND	6 Nov, 2002	Jamshedpur	not out			46	1/0
184.	WI	IND	9 Nov, 2002	Nagpur	run out			51	0/0
185.	WI	IND	12 Nov, 2002	Rajkot	dnb				2/0
186.	WI	IND	15 Nov, 2002	Ahmedabad	not out			109	1/0
187.	WI	IND	18 Nov, 2002	Baroda	caught	Gayle, CH	Samuels, MN	33	1/0

No.	Against	In	Date	Venue	How Out	Fielder	Bowler	Runs	Cts/Sts
188.	WI	IND	21 Nov, 2002	Jodhpur	caught	Powell, RL	Drakes, VC	58	1/0
189.	WI	IND	24 Nov, 2002	Vijayawada	caught	Sarwan, RR	Lawson, JJC	3	0/1
190.	NZ	NZ	26 Dec, 2002	Auckland	caught	Vettori, DL	Tuffey, DR	20	3/0
191.	NZ	NZ	29 Dec, 2002	Napier	run out			18	1/0
192.	NZ	NZ	1 Jan, 2003	Christchurch	caught	Vettori, DL	Hitchcock, PA	20	0/0
193.	NZ	NZ	4 Jan, 2003	Queenstown	bowled		Adams, AR	18	1/0
194.	NZ	NZ	8 Jan, 2003	Wellington	caught	McCullum, BB	Styris, SB	7	1/0
195.	NZ	NZ	11 Jan, 2003	Auckland	lbw		Styris, SB	21	2/0
196.	NZ	NZ	14 Jan, 2003	Hamilton	caught	Styris, SB	Mills, KD	12	0/0
197.	HOL	SA	12 Feb, 2003	Paarl	bowled		de Leede, TBM	17	3/0
198.	AUS	SA	15 Feb, 2003	Centurion	bowled		Gillespie, JN	1	0/1
199.	ZIM	ZIM	19 Feb, 2003	Harare	not out			43	1/0
200.	NAM	SA	23 Feb, 2003	Pietermaritzburg	dnb				2/0
201.	ENG	SA	26 Feb, 2003	Durban	caught	Collingwood, PD	Caddick, AR	62	3/0
202.	PAK	SA	01 Mar, 2003	Centurion	not out			44	1/0
203.	KEN	SA	07 Mar, 2003	Cape Town	c & b	Obuya, CO	Obuya, CO	32	0/0
204.	SL	SA	10 Mar, 2003	Johannesburg	not out			18	1/0
205.	NZ	SA	14 Mar, 2003	Centurion	not out			53	1/0
206.	KEN	SA	20 Mar, 2003	Durban	not out			1	2/0
207.	AUS	SA	23 Mar, 2003	Johannesburg	bowled		Bichel, AJ	47	1/0

Centuries

Runs	*Balls*	*4s/6s*	*Against*	*Venue*	*Date*
107	116	10/0	Pakistan	Chennai	21 May, 1997
123	123	10/1	New Zealand	Taupo	9 Jan, 1999
116	118	12/0	Sri Lanka	Nagpur	22 Mar, 1999
104	109	10/0	Kenya	Bristol	23 May, 1999
145	129	17/1	Sri Lanka	Taunton	26 May, 1999
103	124	8/2	West Indies	Singapore	8 Sep, 1999
153	152	15/2	New Zealand	Hyderabad	8 Nov, 1999
109	124	8/0	West Indies	Ahmedabad	15 Nov, 1999

Wicket	*Runs*	*Partner*	*Against*	*Venue*	*Date*
3rd	161	M Azharuddin	Pakistan	Toronto	17 Sep, 1996
4th	110	M Azharuddin	Australia	Mohali	3 Nov, 1996
4th	105	M Azharuddin	South Africa	Port Elizabeth	2 Feb, 1997
1st	117	SC Ganguly	South Africa	East London	4 Feb, 1997
2nd	130	SC Ganguly	West Indies	St. Vincent	30 Apr, 1997
3rd	134	VG Kambli	Pakistan	Chennai	21 May, 1997
4th	117	M Azharuddin	Sri Lanka	Colombo (RPS)	18 Aug, 1997
3rd	162	Robin Singh	Sri Lanka	Colombo (SSC)	23 Aug, 1997

Wkt	Runs	Partner	Against	Venue	Date
2nd	180	SR Tendulkar	Zimbabwe	Bulawayo	26 Sep, 1998
3rd	140	SR Tendulkar	Australia	Dhaka	28 Oct, 1998
2nd	113	SC Ganguly	New Zealand	Taupo	9 Jan, 1999
2nd	236	SC Ganguly	Sri Lanka	Nagpur	22 Mar, 1999
2nd	166	S Ramesh	Pakistan	Sharjah	13 Apr, 1999
2nd	130	SC Ganguly	South Africa	Hove	15 May, 1999
2nd	318	SC Ganguly	Sri Lanka	Taunton	26 May, 1999
5th	102	Nikhil Chopra	West Indies	Singapore	8 Sep, 1999
2nd	331	SR Tendulkar	New Zealand	Hyderabad	8 Nov, 1999
4th	109	SC Ganguly	Australia	Melbourne	12 Jan, 2000
4th	109	SC Ganguly	Australia	Melbourne	12 Jan, 2000
2nd	180	SR Tendulkar	South Africa	Nagpur	19 Mar, 2000
2nd	180	SR Tendulkar	South Africa	Nagpur	19 Mar, 2000
2nd	145	SC Ganguly	South Africa	Nairobi	13 Oct, 2000
2nd	145	SC Ganguly	South Africa	Nairobi	13 Oct, 2000
2nd	175	SC Ganguly	Zimbabwe	Ahmedabad	5 Dec, 2000
2nd	114	SR Tendulkar	Zimbabwe	Jodhpur	8 Dec, 2000
5th	100	V Sehwag	Australia	Bangalore	25 Mar, 2001
5th	102	Yuvraj Singh	Sri Lanka	Colombo (SSC)	1 Aug, 2001
5th	131*	Yuvraj Singh	England	Lord's	29 Jun, 2002

Wkt	*Runs*	*Partner*	*Against*	*Venue*	*Date*
4th	169	SR Tendulkar	England	Chester-le-Street	4 Jul, 2002
6th	117	Mohd Kaif	Zimbabwe	Colombo (RPS)	14 Sep, 2002
5th	105	VVS Laxman	West Indies	Nagpur	9 Nov, 2002
3rd	103	VVS Laxman	West Indies	Ahmedabad	15 Nov, 2002
4th	129	Mohd Kaif	New Zealand	Centurion	14 Mar, 2003

Statistical Highlights

- Made debut in Ranji Trophy against Maharashtra at Nehru Stadium, Pune on 2 February, 1991 to become the 207th player to represent Karnataka in the National Championships. Scored 82 runs.
- Playing in his 23rd Ranji Trophy match, he led Karnataka for the first time against Tamil Nadu at Bhadravathi on 4 February, 1996.
- Made debut in One Day International match against Sri Lanka at Singapore on 3 April, 1996 becoming the 95th player to represent India. Scored 3 runs.
- Made his debut in Test cricket against England at Lord's on 20 June, 1996 alongwith Saurav Ganguly. He was the 207th player to represent India in tests.
- He became the first Indian batsman to be dismissed in the nineties on test debut. He fell short of 5 runs to join Saurav Ganguly in making a century on debut. In the annals of test cricket history only 24 batsmen earlier to him had failed to notch up a century on debut. For India, the previous highest score by a debutant without reaching a century was 85 runs scored by KC Ibrahim against West Indies at New Delhi in 1948-49.
- Rahul Dravid was presented with a Maruti 800 as a reward for being chosen 'the most valuable player to the Indian team on the tours and Sri Lanka and Canada' by Kothari Products Ltd. The committee which chose him for the award included Kapil Dev, Sunil Gavaskar, Ravi Shastri and Deepak Kothari.
- For the first time, Rahul Dravid scored most runs in the Test Series against South Africa during India's tour in December, 96 to January, 97. He scored 277 runs in 3 tests at an average of 55.40 with one century (148 at Johannesburg).

Series	*Against*	*In*	*Mts*	*Inns*	*Nos*	*Runs*	*HS*	*Avges*	*100s*	*50s*
1996-97	SA	SA	3	6	1	277	148	55.40	1	1
1996-97	WI	WI	5	7	2	360	92	72.00	0	4

- He completed 1000 runs test cricket when he was on 53 in the 5th and final test against West Indies at Bourda Oval, Georgetown, Guyana 17 April, 1997. He was playing in his 14th test and 23rd innings. It was for the second time in his career that he failed to convert his 90s into 100 as he missed a century by 8 runs in this test match.

Index